The
LAKE COUNTIES
of one hundred years ago

HOSPITAL PARADE ON KING STREET, ULVERSTON

CULGAITH FÊTE

The
LAKE COUNTIES
of one hundred years ago

JOHN MARSH & JOHN GARBUTT

ALAN SUTTON PUBLISHING LIMITED

First published in the United Kingdom in 1994 by
Alan Sutton Publishing Ltd • Phoenix Mill • Far Thrupp • Stroud
Gloucestershire

First published in the United States of America in 1994 by
Alan Sutton Publishing Inc. • 83 Washington Street • Dover • NH 03820

British Library Cataloguing in Publication Data

A catalogue record for this book is available from the British Library.

ISBN 0-7509-0382-1

Library of Congress Cataloging in Publication Data applied for

This book is dedicated to the memory of Hardwicke Drummond Rawnsley (1851–1920) who lived through the times depicted
and who, greatly loving the fair things of nature and art, set all his love to the service of God and man.

BUILDING *THE LADY OF THE LAKE*, CONISTON

Typeset in 11/13 Bembo Light.
Typesetting and origination by
Alan Sutton Publishing Limited.
Printed and bound in Great Britain by
WBC, Bridgend, Mid Glam.

Preface

By placing a wealth of carefully chosen and well-reproduced photographs alongside extracts of the good descriptive writing of the years about a hundred years ago we hope to recreate some of the flavour of life in a period only just outside living memory. Our aim is to give the reader an insight into some of the life and times of the people in the late nineteenth and early twentieth century in that amalgam of county areas – Cumberland, Westmorland and Lancashire North of the Sands – that the guidebook writers for over two hundred years have entitled 'The Lake Counties'.

The differences between town and country and between the dress of formal occasions and the workplace immediately provide fascinating comparison. The roads and streets are often empty of the traffic which today we take so much as part of our existence. We notice also, in an area of widely differing communities, the differences between the buildings, the transport and the faces of the people caught for a brief second all those years ago. We may look wistfully at cottages and their occupants and place them in a romantic image of old rural life, but we must not be fooled by appearances which possibly were contrived for the camera. Many homes were cold and damp, lacked proper ventilation or sanitation, were overcrowded, and had no source of instant power. Many inhabitants were poor and the welfare state that we take for granted today was only just in its formation by the early twentieth century. Often good food and domestic comforts were rarely afforded, and 'the workhouse' was a fear carried by many from day to day as ill health and poor wages tested many working-class households. The Lake Counties are famed for their beauty of scene, the connections with the famous and the literate and, in the times depicted, they were the home of many of the new rich produced by Victorian England. The Lake Counties also had their problems in the poor peasant farmers, their exploited miners and quarrymen and their large open spaces which left many having to walk huge distances in order to obtain food, education and religious and medical assistance.

Most of the photographs and text chosen for this book come from the period from the 1880s to the end of the first decade of this century. A few stray just outside these boundaries but are included as they are so typical of the late

BRAYTON COLLIERY SHAFT BOTTOM

FURNESS ABBEY WEST RANGE

Victorian and early Edwardian periods and because they balance the overall picture. To include every town and village in such a geographically wide area would require a book much larger than this, but representations of most areas are included as are the diverse activities of the times. Transport systems are stressed as these were contributing at that time towards the revolution in the Lake Counties as lifestyles nearly a thousand years old were changing towards the society we know today. The transformation of the Lake Counties was undoubtedly a result of changes in transportation.

The photographs chosen come from a large number available from the period taken mainly by the professional photographers who proliferated throughout the whole area from the 1870s. The record they have left is a tribute to their impressive entrepreneurial activities. The collection also includes pictures by such gifted amateurs as Rupert Potter, father of Beatrix Potter, and we are pleased to be able to include some of his previously unpublished photographs.

We are fortunate also in having a good choice of county writers of the period. The Lake Counties, more so than many other counties, have received the attention of famous writers over a lengthy period of time. Rawnsley, Ruskin, Collingwood and many of their contemporaries felt they understood the Lake Counties of their day. John Ruskin also noticed the circumstances of the peasant and the working class he so frequently came in contact with, and this resulted in writings which affected the thinking of many social reformers and educationalists in the first decades of the twentieth century. The mixture of art nouveau paternalism and down-to-earth realism which characterized their approach was quite unique among the reforming influences abroad at the time.

The assembly of the material for this book has given us both a great deal of satisfaction and fun. We have received help from many people who have loaned books and pictures and offered advice and comment as the book progressed. Looking through the photographic collections of others proved just as exciting as the production of the book.

We would like to thank The Trustees of the Armitt Library, Ambleside, George Dawson of the N. Carradice collection, Harry Fancy of the Whitehaven Museum (never too busy in spite of his museum's move to exciting dock-side premises this year), John Fairer of Shap, Iver Gray of Longtown, Richard Hall of the Cumbria County Archive Service, Vera and Malcolm Grinrod of Tilberthwaite, Kath Hayhurst of the Holme & District Local History Society, Neil Honeyman of Barrow, Abigail Reed of Kendal, Peter Robinson of the Cumbrian Railways Association, Barbara Smith of Bewcastle, Marlene and Sydney Storey of Longtown, Anne and Bill Thomas of Seaton, Olive Wilson of Rigmaden, and finally our wives, Barbara and Jean, stoical supporters of our enthusiasm.

JOHN MARSH & JOHN GARBUTT

Introduction

The 'Lake Counties', a title which comes to us from the romantic approach to the area's topography, are now called Cumbria and include the Lake District National Park and various very different areas of the old counties of Cumberland, Westmorland and the Cartmel and Furness districts of Lancashire (or Lancashire north of the sands). Modern Cumbria also includes a part of the old West Riding of Yorkshire around Sedbergh, but this book respects the intentions of the romantic authors of the title 'Lake Counties' and omits what is, in fact, part of the Yorkshire Dales.

This is an area of striking scenery dominated by the central mountains, which are surrounded by fertile plains and river valleys, and the sea, with natural boundaries at the Solway in the north and Morecambe Bay in the south. The Pennines form most of the eastern flank. The district includes one of the country's earliest industrial sites in the Langdale stone axe 'factories' and has the stone circles of a civilization of hunter-gatherer folk about which so little is known. For nearly two thousand years this was border land as rivers and mountains tend to divide communities and thus be used politically as borders. The Roman Wall, one of the world's historic treasures, today attests to use of the border features by the Roman civilization. Later, kingdoms of varying size used the natural borders of the district as protection. The sea in the west was the great natural boundary, but it was also used as the major means of transport until the nineteenth century when land transport began to improve. The mountains and river boundaries were also transport boundaries which were only overcome with difficulty in the years up to the nineteenth century. The early Christians, seeking isolation, found many places in the district to their liking, the most evocative of which must be the lonely cell of Saint Herbert on his island in Derwentwater. The later medieval Church also found the remoteness attractive, and its monasteries were sited in lonely places such as at Furness, Shap and Lanercost. Some of the early Christian sites attracted settlement, and 'church' towns grew which became the modern towns of the area. The Normans on their arrival in the eleventh and twelfth centuries consolidated many such towns and their baronial castles were built to 'protect' the places. It was not until the eighteenth and nineteenth centuries that the town patterns then evolved were radically changed with industrialization. Barrow-in-Furness was a new nineteenth-century 'borough', owing its foundation to industry, and many of the older settlements such as Workington, Whitehaven, Maryport and Carlisle were drastically altered to accommodate the new industries. Some

CARLISLE CASTLE

3

HIGHMOOR, WIGTON

towns became dominated by the industries that were sited in their area, and drifted into industrial slum.

The rural life of the district varied greatly from area to area. Even in quite barren moorlands well-watered valleys gave an agricultural contrast. The great valley of the River Eden and the north Cumberland plain both had fertile land in abundance, while the central mountain area and the fell lands to the east were only able to support grazing. The nineteenth century inherited this pattern of agriculture of centuries before, with farming representing a major part of the economic pattern. The lot of the farm labourer, poor and exploited in the main, changed when the towns of the district offered an alternative in the new factories, shipyards, steelworks and mines. The poverty and exploitation varied only slightly, but the working-class communities of Furness, the Cumberland West Coast and Carlisle possibly offered a safer haven than the weather and landowner. During the depressed years of the turn of the century the Christian Church in its divided form offered succour to most communities in many differing ways, with the Salvation Army standing out then as a supporter of those at the bottom of the communal heap. Many parish churches were in the process of being built, rebuilt or restored as a demand for extra church places was met. 'The church' (or chapel, or mission) was the centre of social as well as spiritual life for many families, with groups such as church youth groups occupying the young in a way to be followed by the Scouts early in the twentieth century. The Temperance movement, born out of the wretched alcohol abuse in the early nineteenth century, was strong in all parts of the Counties but noticeably among the

large Methodist communities of the Eden Valley. In the eighteenth century the Quaker movement had, in many areas, provided a source of support in difficult times, but by the late nineteenth century much had changed with many owners of original Quaker enterprises no longer supporting that sect but adopting Methodism or the new Church of England. The workers who worked for the industries owned by these Christian industrialists were lucky as the communal care associated with them led to greatly different conditions from the exploitation offered by many of the others.

Many of the new rich settlers in the Lake Counties came with a social conscience and offered more to their fellow human beings than being a poor law guardian looking after the local workhouse. Notable among these was John Ruskin who, in fact, had a great effect on events far away from Cumbria as well as changing the local scene with such schemes as the Langdale Linen industry.

Tourism also had a large effect on the turn-of-the-century Lakes Counties as more and more of the local folk became dependent on it for most, if not all, of their income. The railway companies such as the Furness and the London and North Western offered packaged tours as neat and well priced as any today. It was possible to 'do' the central Lake District from Blackpool by boat, charabanc coach and steam yacht in a day. Yorkshire holiday-makers were brought by the boatload to Grange-over-Sands and Arnside. The centre of the Lake District was served by a colliery line so that visitors from the south, north-east and north could visit Keswick and Cockermouth with ease. Hotels, often built by the railway companies, sprang up to support this influx of travellers, and a

BUCK HILL COLLIERY, NEAR GREAT BROUGHTON

SILLOTH HOLIDAY

FREEZE UP AT GREENODD, 1895

sizeable infrastructure of boarding houses, catering establishments, gift shops, and coaching and boating enterprises appeared to provide for the holiday-makers. Wordsworth had died protesting against popular tourism but events could not be stopped. The National Trust was founded in 1893 when Canon Hardwicke Rawnsley, anxious to preserve the beauty of the lakes, involved others, including the Duke of Westminster, and formed a society to preserve 'Places of historic interest and natural beauty'. The opening of the first property acquired in the Lake District, Brandlehow, Derwentwater, is described by Eleanor Rawnsley:

The Princess Louise, Duchess of Argyll, consented to come to dedicate Brandlehow to the use and enjoyment of the public, an engagement which she bravely kept on October 16th, 1902, when instead of the serenity and calm described by Hardwicke Rawnsley in a sonnet, there raged a hurricane of wind and rain. Two hours before H.R.H. arrived, the great marquee, in which she was to be received, went up in the sky like a balloon and came down a wreckage of snapped masts and poles. Miss Octavia Hill has

recorded her impression: 'The scene was most beautiful and very funnily primitive. The great tent was blown to atoms, and the little red dais was out under the free sky with the great lake and splendid mountains and golden bracken slopes around us, and the nice North country people quite near and so happy and orderly.'

The weather was always a problem, with some areas such as Stainmore and Borrowdale being almost dominated by it. The ample supply of water brought water engineers to seek the site of reservoirs, and the tourist industry could only make a joke of what to many farmers was a life or death subject. The winters at the turn of the century were generally harder than today, which made for many great difficulties in an already wretched life and for others great fun as the area became a 'winter resort'. Some skated on frozen lakes as others dug out and fed their life's investment.

Rail transport had transformed all parts of the Counties thirty to fifty years earlier and it comes as some surprise to discover that Kendal might have been what Crewe became. Barrow-in-Furness had its own railway company which served

RAVENSTONEDALE STATION

PHOTOGRAPHERS' VANS AT WHITE MOSS, RYDAL

KENTS BANK STATION

MARY PEPPER LACEMAKING

the surrounding district in goods, mineral and passenger traffic. Carlisle, ancient border city and the site of the only cathedral in the Counties, became a railway town with junctions for many separate railway companies. The craze for railways was fought when it intruded on the beautiful parts of the district and many ideas such as Windermere–Ambleside–Keswick, the branch through Ennerdale, and the Braithwaite to Buttermere routes came to naught, while in other parts the railway opened up a way of life quite unique to isolated communities. The centre of many a village became the station and the goods sidings. The stationmaster joined the vicar as head of the community.

Photography, born in the middle of the nineteenth century, continued to improve and change when in the late 1890s a new media came into use in the form of the picture postcard. In only a decade postcards in a form approved by the Post Office became a major source of communication, almost like the telephone call of today, and were also used as greeting cards at Christmas and birthdays. Holiday-makers sent the 'Wish you were here' greetings. In one of the photographs taken by local postcard producer Atkinson of Ulverston, Mary Pepper, who posed for the artist Millais as the little girl in his painting *Cherry Ripe*, can be seen working at her lace pillow as part of the Ruskin Langdale Linen industry started by her grandmother. People started collecting these pictures and it is from such collections that many of our illustrations have come, preserved by chance from the dustbin or the bonfire. These survivors and other pictures saved in albums in differing formats such as carte-de-visite, cabinet or full plate now tell us much of their age in *The Lake Counties of one hundred years ago*.

The LAKE COUNTIES

of one hundred years ago

ULVERSTON HOSPITAL PARADE

COCKERMOUTH

FAIRS & MARKETS – CUMBERLAND

Alston – Fairs on the third saturday in March for cattle; saturday before April 23 for horses, cattle and sheep; the last thursday in May for horses, cattle, sheep and pigs; the saturday on or before September 27, for horses and cattle; saturday on or before October 18 for sheep, and the first thursday in November for horses, cattle and sheep

Brampton – Fairs for sheep and cattle, on April 20, the second wednesday after Whitsuntide, the second wednesday in September, and the third friday in October. Hirings and pleasure fairs are held on Whit Wednesday and on the first wednesday after November 11

Carlisle – A Hiring fair is held on saturday before Whitsunday, on saturday nearest November 11, and on saturday before Candlemas and Lammas; fairs are also held on April 22 for cattle, and on August 26 for horses, cattle and sheep; and on September 19 for cattle, sheep and lambs; and similar fairs on the last three saturdays of October and on saturday nearest November 11. When April 22, August 26, or September 19, fall on a sunday, the marts hold the fair on the saturday preceding. Market days, Wednesday and Saturday; the latter, which is the principal market, is remarkably well attended

Cockermouth – Fairs are held on Whit-Monday and Martinmas Monday for hiring of servants, and every fortnight, commencing in May, for cattle. Market day, Monday. Cattle fairs, wednesday after April 12, first wednesday in May (the spring fair), and every alternate wednesday in May; also a monthly sale of horses on the first friday in the month, except in February and October, when it is held on February 17, and the second tuesday in October. An annual sale of bulls and store stock of every description is held on the last friday in March; the special sale of tup lambs is held on the last friday in August; lamb sales second monday in September; annual ram sale and store stock of every description on the last friday in September; special sale of store stock of every description on the second wednesday in October; the annual autumn bull sale on the last friday in October, and the prize show and sale of fat cattle at Christmas

Egremont – Fairs for the sale of cattle and horses on February 17, the third friday in May and June 5. Hirings for servants take place on saturday at Whitsuntide and Martinmas. Crab fair, held September 18, is for horses, sheep and cattle

11

BROUGH HILL FAIR

Eskdale (Boot) – A pleasure fair, and a cattle and sheep fair are held here on the second monday in September, and a ram show is held at the Woolpack inn on the last friday in September

Gosforth – Fairs at Boonwood for the sale of cattle on April 25 and October 18. Hiring fairs, for servants, are held at Gosforth at Whitsuntide and Martinmas

Keswick – Fairs first saturday in October, and on the first thursday after May 1st, and the two subsequent alternate thursdays for cattle; a fair for rams and cheese on the saturday after October 29, and the hirings for servants at Whitsuntide and Martinmas

Kirkoswald – A fair is held on the 5th August (St Oswald's Day)

Maryport – Market day, friday; fairs on the friday before Whitsunday and the friday before November 2

Millom – Market day, saturday

Penrith – Market day, tuesday

Ravenglass – Fairs for cattle May 6, June 8 and August 5

Rosley – Horse and cattle fairs on Whit Monday and two alternate mondays after these fairs

Nether Wasdale – Sheep and pleasure fair on the first monday in September

Whitehaven – Markets are held on tuesday, thursday and saturday; thursday is the principal market day

Wigton – Market every tuesday in the open street for corn and all kinds of farm produce, and on St Thomas's Day is also a very large one for meat, apples and honey. Fairs are held on February 20, for horses and cattle, which was formerly one of the largest in this part of the country; and on April 5 for cattle and merchandise; and Whit-Tuesday and Martinmas Tuesday for hiring agricultural servants

Workington – Market days wednesday and saturday, fairs are held on Whit-Wednesday and the wednesday after November 11

Kelly's Directory, 1897

CARLISLE

SHEEP WASHING, MERENESS, CARTMEL

FARMING

The following table shows the acreage under each kind of crop, and the number of horses, cattle, sheep and pigs in the County of Cumberland, as taken from the Agricultural Returns, 1895:

Crops	Acres
Corn and cereals	85,880
Roots, artificial grasses, cabbage and rape	46,220
Clover and grasses	115,654
Permanent pasture	330,105
Bare fallow	1,211
Orchards	380
Market gardens	425
Nursery grounds	223
Woods and plantations	35,054

Live Stock	Number
Horses for agriculture, brood mares and unbroken horses	22,542
Cows in milk or calf	45,941
Other cattle	95,996
Sheep, 1 year old	341,469
Ditto, under 1 year	176,807
Pigs	23,708

Cumberland contained in 1891, inhabited houses	52,361
Civil parishes	201
Rateable value	£1,597,226
Mountain and heath land used for grazing, acres	252,562
Total acreage of the County	970,161

Kelly's Directory, 1897

HOW TO GROW GRASS

The after-management during the summer is a matter of extreme importance, and to justify our proposal of the management it must be remembered that on the surface the land not having been disturbed much we do not expect many weeds to appear, as they would on a regular fallow surface, therefore we advise that the young plants, together with any old ones which may have escaped during the working and seeding, should be allowed to grow up together until there is food enough to turn in some young store cattle. Care should be taken not to allow any sheep to feed on the land until the second year after seeding, nor should the young cattle be allowed to feed until the grasses are strong, and the longer it is deferred the better until the grasses will be rooted firmly enough to prevent their being pulled up. The feeding should not be long continued, only sufficient to pull off the tallest blades of grass. In some cases it may even be advisable to run the mowing machine over and take off any weeds and all grasses which may have run up, and then leave the young grass until necessity compels the feeding by young cattle, but dairy cows will sometimes be too strong and heavy treading for young seeds. If the land is very poor then to the manure which is to be applied, 15 bushels or 20 bushels of damp ashes should be mixed with the manures, which prevent their flying before the wind at sowing time, also tend to the more regular distribution of the manure. Still, in the next year, if the seeds

THE AMBLESIDE GARDENER

HOLME GROUND, TILBERTHWAITE, CONISTON

SEASCALE STATION

do not appear strong, they should again be manured with a similar mixture of manures, or a mixture of earthy composts and dung, but more especially may this be necessary in the case of pastures having been overrun with moss, for except in those cases where the pasture has been recently made and the deficiences have occurred through some of the plants having died out, we may be quite sure that the necessity for renovating has been caused by the land being too poor for producing the grasses indigenous to the soil. With regard to the seeds to be sown to renovate pastures which have failed to maintain a plant of grass sufficient to make a turf, we must of course take notice of the soil to be seeded, as there may be a partial or half a plant of the old or formerly seeded and survived plants. In case of those pastures which have been entirely cultivated on the surface to destroy moss or couch, then we of course recommend for renovating the pasture so far as it is required by the entire loss and vacancy of the original turf, that the whole of the mixtures and quantities of each grass seeds should be used, just as if we were laying down for a permanent pasture on a fallow in the first instance.

Jackson's Ulverston & North Lonsdale Almanac & Tide Table for 1885

DATUR HORA QUIETI (1889–1899)

But it shall come to pass, that at evening time it shall be light.
ZECH. xiv. 7.

In the summer of 1889, at Seascale, on the Cumberland coast, Mr Ruskin was still busy upon 'Praeterita.' He had his task planned out to the finish: in nine more chapters he meant to conclude his third volume with a review of the leading memories of his life, down to the year 1875, when the story was to close. Passages here and there were written, material collected from old letters and journals, and the contents and titles of the chapters arranged; but the intervals of strength had become fewer and shorter, and at last, in spite of all his courage and energy, he was brought face to face with the fact that his powers were ebbing away, and that head and hand would do their work no more.

He could not finish 'Praeterita'; but he could not leave it without record of one companionship of his life, which was, it seemed, all that was left to him of the old times and the old folks at home. And so, setting aside the plans he had made, he devoted the last chapter, as his forebodings told him it must be, to his cousin, Mrs Arthur Severn, and wrote the story of 'Joanna's Care.'

In his bedroom at Seascale, morning after morning, he still worked, or tried to work, as he had been used to do on journeys farther afield in brighter days. But now he seemed lost among the papers scattered on his table; he could not fix his mind upon them, and turned from one subject to another in despair; and yet patient, and kindly to those with him whose help he could no longer use, and who dared not show – though he could not but guess – how heart-breaking it was.

They put the best face upon it, of course: drove in the afternoons about the country – to Muncaster Castle, to Calder Abbey, where he tried to sketch once more; and when the proofs of 'Joanna's Care' were finally revised, to Wastwater. But travelling now as no longer restorative. . . .

In August, after his return to Coniston, the storm-cloud came down upon him once more. It was only in the summer of 1890 that he was able to get about. But firmly convinced that his one chance lay in absolute rest and quiet, he has since wisely refused any sort of exertion, and has been rewarded by a steady improvement in health and strength.

W.G. Collingwood

AN EARLY MOUNTAIN RESCUE

The famous rainbow-tinted Screes are on our right hand; next is Lingmell; then the pikes of Scafell, (3,166 feet), and then Scafell itself. These pikes are the highest land in England, and much sought after by the ambitious pedestrian, although not always

WASTWATER

JOHN RUSKIN

found. It was in the summer of 1859 that, coming over from Borrowdale to Wastdale, over Sty Head, in our walking costume, we overtook a young gentleman attired as though for a lounge in Bond Street; shirt-collar had he, an umbrella-parasol, and (if we do not exaggerate) straps! yes, he was bent upon ascending Scafell Pike in straps!! After that little walk, he said, he hoped to have the pleasure of meeting us that evening at William Ritson's, one of the excellent farm houses at Wastdale; whereto we replied something civil, but very much doubted in our inmost heart of the event's coming off. When we told one of the dalesmen what this superlatively dressed person was about to attempt, he pulled his pipe out of his contemptuous lips, and said 't' lad el dee,' – meaning that it would be the death of him. When mist came on that evening, in such thick folds that Wastdale might have been Salisbury Plain for all that we could see of the mountains, the good dalesman and some friends of his started to feel their way up those pikes. They found poor Straps, dead beat, but upon the very summit of the hill, lying down breathless upon his back, and watching the awful curtain of night and death descending upon him. It was so dark that even the dalesmen themselves lost their way in coming down, and carried the poor young gentleman into Eskdale. The Wastdale folk will do any kind thing for any body.

England's Lakeland – a tour therein

SUNNY BANK, TORVER

PRACTICAL GUIDE TO THE LAKE DISTRICT

A few words of advice to the tourist on his dress and equipment will not be unacceptable, to beginners at least.

If the tourist works out the programme comprised in the following pages, he will find a knapsack indispensable. It is possible to so contrive matters that luggage can be sent ahead by coach or rail, but, to say nothing of the risk of loss or delay, such a plan limits the traveller to the high roads. He who means to stay all night at Wastwater or Haweswater, or crosses from Ullswater to Rosthwaite, must carry his baggage with him or dispense with baggage altogether, a thing which the author has never succeeded in doing.

Carrying a knapsack then, the tourist is advised to get one with a wicker frame, so constructed as to keep the knapsack entirely off the back. Let it also have a comfortable handle at the upper end, that the shoulders may be occasionally relieved by the knapsack being carried in the hand. While coming down steep hills it is best to carry the knapsack in this way, as doing so steadies the walker remarkably.

As to its contents, these must be to a large extent left to the choice of the individual. A flask of spirits should not be omitted, and a small case containing needles and thread, pins, small buttons, and a coil of whipcord, is a desirable addition. The tourist must, of course, carry *quant. suff.* of haberdashery, and in particular should not omit dry socks or stockings, as many fell tops are boggy and damp. It will also be wise to find room, if possible, for a knitted 'Cardigan' wool vest. Considerable variations of temperature are certain to be encountered, and, a heavy overcoat being out of the question, the Cardigan will take its place efficiently and advantageously.

CLIMBERS ON PAVEY ARK, LANGDALE

ARMATHWAITE

The tourist will, of course, have a light macintosh strapped to his knapsack. It will be advisable to take a pair of thin macintosh knickerbockers to protect the legs, unless a knickerbocker suit is worn, when this will be unnecessary.

He must take a compass, and one or two squares of the ordnance map, pasted on cloth and folded. He should also take a whistle, to attract attention in case of accident. The author has found a whistle useful before now when lost in the mist, between Rossett Ghyll and Stae Head!·

A walking stick, or Alpenstock, will complete the list of accessories. The former is the most generally useful; the latter is of service on very broken ground, or in ascending or descending steep hill sides; but, in the average of the day's work, the walking stick is the most serviceable. In certain places (on Striding Edge for instance, or in one or two clefts and gullies on Scawfell Pikes) even a walking stick is a temporary hindrance.

As to dress, the author's experience is that so much depends on the time of the year and individual physique, that only general advice can be given. Strong laced boots, with double soles, should be worn. The ground between Langdale and Buttermere would cut light single soled boots to pieces. The underclothing should consist exclusively of flannel or woollen. Oxford collars (Shakespeares) will be found convenient, as one will last for several days (paper ones must on no account be worn). If a knickerbocker suit be worn, leggings of any kind may be left at home. On the other hand, knickerbocker stockings expose the legs and feet unpleasantly to dust and dirt.

The head gear worn by the author has usually been either a Scotch cap or a common felt hat.

The author dares not venture to advise lady pedestrians as to costume, further than by saying that they should wear woollen stockings, strong well-made boots, and woollen dresses, light or heavy, according to the time of the year.

One last word on the subject of tourists' dress. Avoid absurdities, eccentricities, and whimsicalities of costume. They don't promote your pleasure, and they interfere more or less with that of others, besides bringing into disrepute the genus 'pedestrian tourist,' for whose use and behoof this book has been written.

·*Commonly written Sty Head.*

J.L. Moore

18

BROUGHTON-IN-FURNESS

FROM THIRLMERE TO KESWICK BY COACH

We are in a vale of sounding waters, a valley with a swift watershed, Manchester chose well. . . . Those few houses by the dark firs are still called Wythburn City. There are earthwork remains there that look as if earlier settlers than our Viking forefathers had chosen that spot for their 'sitting.' . . .

'Eight miles from Keswick, sir; if you want the best walk in these parts you will turn in the gate there, back by where them waterworks gentlemen is making all that smother with the engine, and get along on foot toward the city, and keep on the old pack-horse road to Armboth House, and so along west of the mere, and join the main road at Bridge End, beyond Great How. Finest walk in these parts; and the worst of it is, them Manchester folk are not allowed to leave it alone. You see that bit of a house end covered with ivy; that's the Cherry Tree. Wordsworth wrote a bit of po'try about that.' I remembered that the Waggoner had stopped there, and had a good two hours of easy fun, for the villagers had met for dance and frolic. It was 'the village merry night.' Ah, days of Merrie England – days when for such merry nights every clown in these Cumbrian valleys had been put through his paces, and could, so one is told, dance a three-cornered reel fit for a king to look upon – when will ye return? The fiddlers are gone. 'Jack's the laddie,' the favourite tune, is heard no more, and the dancing master has been put to flight by H.M. Inspector and payment by results.

MAY DAY, TEMPLE SOWERBY

19

SEDGWICK POST OFFICE

We pass Birkett's picturesque little post-office, smothered in cotoniaster; go beneath the hideous wooden bridge erection that carries the trollies of the waterwork excavators to the tip at the great embankment of refuse close by the sluice that will one day open its mouth and set the Thirlmere waters streaming deeply underground, and along far heights and through distant meadows to far-off, thirsty Manchester; and our eyes are straining now to catch sight of –

> An upright mural block of stone,
> Moist with pure water trickling down.

For beside the road, where it runs parallel with and close above the shore of the lake, stands the 'Rock of Names' . . . At this rock six poets –

> Meek women, men as true and brave
> As ever went to a hopeful grave –

worked to engrave their initials in full trust that –

> The loved rock would keep
> The charge when they were laid asleep.

Their names were William Wordsworth, Mary Hutchinson (afterwards Mrs Wordsworth), Dorothy Wordsworth, Samuel Taylor Coleridge, John Wordsworth, and Sarah Hutchinson. Mercifully for the engravers, the moss, fed by the water trickling down, obscured their handiwork. If local gossip is to be believed, a stalwart dalesman added his own initials, W.W.,

in pure ignorance of the company he was in, and has only lately discovered that he had joined the sacred choir.

Alas, for the march of time and the necessities of contractors, since this last sentence was penned news reached the writer from headquarters that the contractor wished to exploit the 'Rock of Names,' on the chance of getting suitable stone for use in building some of the waterwork walls; and rather than allow the rock to be blown to bits, he obtained leave of the Manchester Waterworks Committee to attempt the removing of the rock bodily. This was found to be an impossibility. The nature of the rock, which was really of the nature of glass – being lava and volcanic ash – and glass that had been cracked and splintered in the process of cooling – prevented anything like a wholesale removal. A 'plug and feather' was called into requisition, and the surface of the rock was thus removed piecemeal. It is hoped that the pieces will be able to be put together much as one puts a puzzle together, and bedded in Portland cement. It is possible that it may, even in its mutilated condition, rest upon the side of the new road at the higher level, and serve to keep alive the memory of the dead that made it famous.

A few paces forward, and we are rumbling by Clark's Loup or Leap. 'You know the story, sir,' a gentleman said, who had got up on the coach at Wythburn, and who was evidently a native; 'a man named Clark got so jealous of his wife, he told her he had resolved to put an end to his life. She dissuaded him from hanging himself, saying it was painful; from shooting himself, urging that he might possibly not kill himself outright. He proposed death by drowning; this seemed to please her, and they came together to Thirlmere side. He said he would wade in. She told him to remember that the water was cold, and he would give himself needless pain. Walking on, they reached this rock. This would suit him, the wife said, for the water was deep enough for the purpose. Clark was about to throw himself in when Madam bade him remember that, unless he took a run and a leap, he might injure himself seriously upon the rocks below. He took her advice, put off his coat, solemnly ran, solemnly leapt, solemnly sank. She solemnly waited till he disappeared, and then walked solemnly home, feeling that she had done no more nor less than any good wife should do – had given the best advice she could under the circumstances. You may smile, but the writer of the 'Survey of the Lakes in 1789,' who tells us the story, conversed with the woman and heard it verified from her own lips.'

'It's a valley full of old-world interest,' continued the narrator. 'Yonder, across the lake just opposite, under Bull Crags, is Justice Stone, where, in the olden time, the inhabitants met to arrange quarrels and administer law. There is a Web Stone high on the Fell, too, where the Thirlmere folk left their homespun or their yarns for the poor, plague-stricken dwellers in the Keswick Valley. Not far from that most beautiful of Thirlmere waterfalls, Launcy Ghyll – called, doubtless, after some Launcelot of former fame – is the Rocking Stone; and there, among the larches is the garth of the deer – Deer guards. Newlands had its Hindscarth, Thirlmere its Deergarth.' The coachman smiled and said, 'We call a door hereabout a deer; it was just garden-door happen – but these gentlemen are always finding out something fresh,

MRS TURNER, KENDAL

you know, sir. Will you mind walking up the hill, it's rather a stiff one? Sorry to trouble you; when the new road is made we shall be able to let you keep your seats!'

Up the hill we walked, and were rewarded by the view of that ebon-coloured lake below us, and away to its tiny bridges opposite the solid, genial-looking Armboth Hall, that shone whitely on its garden lawn. . . .

Poets have gazed on Thirlmere and been borne heavenward on the wings of their sweet song. Hither Faber came more than once – he who in his poem 'Thirlmere' tells us,

> All hope, all joy, all mortal life
> With such sweet sadness is inlaid,

found that this cold, blue lake and yonder pine clad Ravencragg, laid a nameless sorrow on his soul. He tells us,

> And I have ridden to the Lake this day
> With more than common gladness,
> But hill and flood upon me strangely weigh
> With new and fearful sadness.

Perhaps, if he were here to-day and walked along through the Dalehead pastures and saw how the exigencies of our time, with its vast centralisation, have obliged Manchester to come and cut away the tall dark pines and (as a bribe to the local

LEECE

THE KINGS HEAD, THIRLSPOT

hotel-keepers and to burke opposition) to offer unconditionally and to be bound by an Act of Parliament – from which nothing but another Act could set it free – to cut away the tall dark crags near Bull Ghyll and run a perfectly level and embanked road right across the western fellside face so that, for twelve weeks in the year, the char-a-banc may rattle in careless merry-go-round where the real lovers of scenery wished to be allowed in quiet to commune with nature – he also would have felt 'this hill and flood upon him weigh with more than common sadness.' But Manchester, though it made ill-advisedly at the time of getting the Thirlmere Waterworks Bill an offer of this second unnecessary public coach road along the heights, is to be absolved. It repented heart and soul and offered to give to England and lovers of English scenery a respite to the fell; offered to make a carriage drive with passes in it all the way from Shoulthwaite Moss to Wythburn on the lines of the old cart track; offered to give a carriage ferry at the Narrows, which would have been, to all dwellers in the locality and all visitors, a priceless boon, if only the public would allow the temporary respite; but those who are supposed to get their living by catering for the convenience of travellers, did not see why the travellers should have a chance of getting across Thirlmere at the Narrows, or why they should wish to escape from a coach road and take their quiet enjoyment in one of the finest pleasure grounds

ever offered to the public for such pleasure and quietude, as this was offered, by Manchester; so Manchester withdrew its offer to the nation. What else could be done?

Well at the top of the hill, a new surprise is opened to us – Skiddaw's double cone far away to the left, Great How in middle distance, and the Naddle Fell making another gateway in the dale, through which, into far distance, runs the lovely Vale of St John; blue Blencathra filling all the distance to the north, and the eye coming back along the brown heights of Helvellyn, by Castle Rock, and the long white Thirlspot or Thrispot Inn, to the magnificent Brown Cove Crags above our heads to the right. It is from here that we get an idea of the way in which the winds and streams and snows have modelled Helvellyn's mountain-side.

Great Dodd, Watson's Dodd, Stybarrow Dodd, and Whiteside seem separated by individual summits and individual torrents. That little outstanding crag, somewhat like a wart upon the sky-line, away beyond the Castle Rock, has an interest. It is still called 'Watch' Crag, and tells a tale of border war and beacon fires. On our left, as we gallop down the hill towards the inn, is the remains of the old school-house – a byre today; further on, the gate that leads to the ancient home of the Leathes, who seem to have dispossessed the Viking Thorold of his name for the mere, and to have called the Brack or Braikmere of their day Leatheswater. Their

CONISTON POST OFFICE

beautiful old house with its great dark oaken stair and its wondrous kitchen fireplace is in the hands now of the Manchester Corporation, and is still hospitable as of old. But the days are gone when the quiet afternoons upon the garden lawn of Dalehead Hall were full of the fun of Robert Southey and the serious talk of the Rydal poet, and the simple common-sense and benevolent projects of William Calvert.

We pull up at the 'King's Head.' The coachman wants his meal, and the horses want their meal and water. What a bit of old Cumberland the half-farm, half-inn, truly is! The yew-tree and the sycamore shadow it from behind, the stream runs bravely for the stable-boy's bucket beside us, and there, in one long line of radiant hospitality and use, under one long roof-tree and with one unbroken front, stand stable, coachhouse, post-office, bar, best parlour, livery-house, lodging-house, and barn.

But, as at the famous 'Swan,' so here at the 'King's Head,' modern landlords have not been wise. The quaintest sign that was ever hung has been discarded, and we can no longer read, as we used to read, the simple truth and simple invitation –

> John Standley lives here and sells good ale,
> Come in and drink before it goes stale;
> John succeeded his uncle Peter,
> In t'old man's time it was never better.

Away we go – the St John's Vale, with its blue Blencathra background, a veritable Lauterbrunnen Pass in miniature before us.

On our left the Dalehead meadows, in which of old stood 'Willie How,' the famous inn-of-call for pack-horse men from Whitehaven to Lancaster. We have forgotten Thirlmere, but Thirlmere is with us all the way, quietly sleeping in the shadow of Raven Crag, just over the brow of Dalehead Park. On our right, beneath its fir-trees, stands a pink-stuccoed lodging-house, four-square. That is the Dalehead post-office, and behind it, thunders down the Brotto Ghyll.

Fisher Place the coachman calls it, but he does not seem to know that Rossetti the poet spent some weeks of the last autumn of his life there, and that a letter in the poet's hand hangs framed upon the walls of the little front room. Poor Rossetti, striken unto death, the landlady there still calls to mind your deep, melodious voice as you paced the little room, reading aloud the last proof of your sonnets! And we who read your letter see what deep impression on other minds than the mind of the Wizard of the North this part of the Thirlspot Valley made.

'The scenery is the most romantic and beautiful that can be conceived, and the retirement more absolute than I ever met with before' – so wrote Rossetti from Fisher Place.

That thin zigzag line upon the hill 'twixt Fisher Place and the next ghyll, 'Stanah,' where the old-fashioned farmhouse, Stanah, stands, is the miners' path that leads to the Styx Pass – as it has been misspelt, for it takes its name from the sticks or stakes that guide the men across the heights and there is nothing Stygian about the upland path to-day – and so over Helvellyn to Patterdale and Ullswater, Glenridding Screes, and far Glencoign. The shepherds of Helvellyn know that

COTTAGES AT CARK

path as well as the Glenridding miners. Up that path, on the first Monday after the 20th of July, they go to hold their annual shepherds' meeting on Stybarrow Dodd. Thither to solemn assembly they climb, taking with them any stray sheep that may have wandered from their neighbours' heaf or pasturage to their own; and there in good fellowship they give and take back the lost children of their various mountain flocks and discuss the affairs of their honourable world of fleece and fatness and friendly self-government. It is worth while noting that Stanah Ghyll – 'Stane Ea' or stone water – has insisted upon the dalesmen paying attention to its swollen tide in the meadows. The banks are built up either side with tons of cobble stones, but it is not only rushing streams in time of heavy rain or melting of the snow that the good people of Legburthwaite have to fear. On August 22, 1749, a waterspout broke on Helvellyn, which denuded the whole of the mountainside, from here as far as eye can see up St John's Vale, of its grass, filled the narrow meadow bottoms with rocks and rubbish, swept Fornside clear of trees, and totally destroyed the Legburthwaite Mill, which used to stand in the mill ghyll just beyond Castle Crag. The very millstones were washed away, and one was never recovered.

But we forget all that wreck, for the green herb has clomb the heights, and the fields are filled with ox-eye daisies and purple cranesbill, and the little How Beck at our side is crystal-clear. Now, on our right, the Castle Rock shines out as bald as the day the waterspout swept it bare. It used to be called Green Crags, but it will never have that name again. Thither the affrighted people from the ruined cottages near took refuge from the appalling water-flood. They hardly knew that in prehistoric days their fore-elders had taken refuge there before them, from the torrents of war. Yet there are signs that armed men have held their camp there in time of trouble.

As we neared Thirlspot just now, Castle Rock stood out like a lion pawing to get free from the mountain side; now it has sunk back into the hill side, and it requires all Sir Walter Scott's magic to bring back

> The mound with airy turrets crowned,
> Buttress and rampires' circling bound,
> And mighty keep and tower.

where the bridal of Triermain was celebrated, and where Gwendolen and Arthur held proud festival. But at times, when the level light strikes up the narrow valley of St John, the rock is fired with gold, and it needs but little imagination to give us back the glory of an enchanted hold.

On our left is rising the tree-covered, fern-swathed height which Wordsworth's

> Three rosy-cheeked schoolboys, the highest not more
> Than the height of a councillor's bag,

chose to climb – and there, dark against the sky, is a facsimile of the 'Maen,' or 'Man,' as the cairns are called in this old

BELL HOUSE, DALTON, BURTON-IN-KENDAL

corner of Little Britain, that without mortar or lime they built at the top of the crag.

Up the brow of the Smithy Hill we go at a sharp canter, and down and over the queer crooked bridge that spans the shining Bure.

Away flits the ring-ousel, or dipper, above the lily leaves that lie upon the quiet, amber-coloured pool; and thanking heaven that we sat fast, as the coachman bade us, we breathe a little more freely – for the passage of that bridge was a doubtful pleasure – and can look behind us upon one of the sweetest pastoral scenes we have yet set eyes on.

The Bure shines and winks at the pretty, single-arched Cumberland bridge. The Bure shines and sings at the stepping-stones. A picturesque farmhouse, with its white porch almost laughing a welcome at us, gleams whitely against the green background of the once wooded Great How. It was tree-covered when I wrote these lines: it is tree-covered no more. The Manchester Corporation, with consummate short sight, have bared the eastern slope to the summit, and cut the woods, whose timber was of no value, smick smooth. They know not what they do who so disrobe a hill in mid vale of its glory, and rob it of its power to give joy and to impress the mind of the passer by. The confusion of gables of the outhouses would detain any artist. The history of the queer Norwegian-looking barn end nearest the road would enchant an archaeologist. For that is the spinning shed. There, in the last century and the beginning of this, the farm folk gathered when the twilight fell; and there, by light of simple rush and home-made candles, the wool they had piled up in the one end of the barn was spun into web and woven into frieze. . . .

Into the hummocky, picturesquely broken ground upon our left a rough road strikes; that is the old packhorse road that used to lead the jangling mules either to the ford, and so to Willie How, near Dalehead, or on under Raven Crag along the west side of Thirlmere.

The spring the mules and packmen drank from still fills the roadside trough a little further on, and the place of the rude cross – at which, who knows, they muttered prayer for safety on their lonely way – may be recognised. At any rate, there, by the roadside, is deeply cut a cross on a boulder stone, which said boulder stone was, when Clarke made his survey of the Lakes a hundred years ago, standing on the right hand side of the then road upon a mound, and was known as Adam's Cross, though even at that time its origin and use had been forgotten. . . .

Now we have won 'the smooth, unpathwayed plain' of Shoulthwaite Moss –

> Where no disturbance comes to intrude
> Upon the pensive solitude.

Nay, this is not strictly true either, for here, just opposite the Bend, as the hill on our left hand is called, purple with shales, and green with streamers of larch that struggle up the height – here, if but the coachman be persuaded to blow his horn, we shall have such mountain music betwixt High Rigg and the

HIGH STREET, WHITEHAVEN

'Ern' or Eagle Crags of Bleaberry Fell as will astonish any pensive one, and people any solitude.

Round to the left we go, with the 'echo dying, dying, dying.' Backwards we look; it is hence that, over the moss, fragrant with the young birch and the breath of the 'sweet gale,' Great How shows to best purpose, and the eye, ranging upwards, catches sight of the highest point of huge Helvellyn. The 'comb of the wild cat's ladder,' as some assert 'Catchedecam' to mean, shows darkly aloft for a moment, and in another moment we have whisked round the corner to the right to catch our first fair sight of Skiddaw's hornéd hill, with Latrigg lying like a cub at its mother's side.

On now, till a sharp turn to the left gives us ample view of the Naddle Vale, so boulder-strewn, so treeless, that it looks almost as if a waterspout had been at work, and it is not till we have turned once more to the right over Rougha Bridge that we find the stone walls have given place to hedges of such rich wild roses and wild-service bush and bird-cherry trees as to recall the dream of paradise, and banish the thought of desolation.

Just before reaching Rougha or Rough How Bridge, had we been here on a certain day nigh fifty years ago, we should have seen the Whitehaven mail come round the corner, crash into a pony-chaise with two middle-aged men in it, have seen the pony-chaise, occupants and all, fly over – or rather through – the wall, and have heard one of the gentleman pick himself up and say, in a solemn way, 'I shall have this matter thoroughly investigated.'

'AWD COOPER', MALLERSTANG POSTMAN, KIRKBY STEPHEN

WHITEHAVEN HARBOUR IN WINTER

We should have heard David Johnson, the driver – pale as death, and pulling up sharp and looking over his shoulder – say, 'Good God! its Maister Wadswuth.'

And, had we been in the Keswick market-place that night, and asked whether Mr Wordsworth was much hurt, we should have heard David Say, 'No, sir, thank Heaven for that, sir! But I never heard a body's tongue swear, gladlier though, for I thowt we'd kilt the poït.'

As confirming this story, the writer may mention that he was driving by the spot the other day with the Archbishop of York, and mentioned the incident. 'Dear me,' said his Grace, 'You recall a drive I had years ago with the very driver of the identical coach. I was a lad coming from school, on my way to my home at Whitehaven, and just here Johnson told me of the collision he had had with Wordsworth's pony carriage, and of the anger of the poet. He further told me how the accident happened. It seems that his off-wheeler tossed his head and got the bit entangled in the pole hook; in consequence, Johnson lost control, and the accident as they came down the incline was unavoidable.' . . .

Nothing now but roses, roses, all the way, till, facing one of the oldest, mossiest dry walls in the country, the humble little parsonage of St John's Vale greets us, standing close to the turn that takes us across the valley to Naddle Fell. The next farmhouse upon our left has historic significance in its name. It is Causeway Foot. Hither ran the Roman road from Penrith, and, from the Roman camp beyond, soldiers passed to and from their camp on Castrigg of to-day. That Miregate road, deep-trodden into the hillside, has seen centuries of travellers passing up to the camp for protection. Up and down that old packhorse road have plied the horses laden with wood

FURNESS ABBEY NAVE

27

CROSTHWAITE, KESWICK

or black plumbago from Borrowdale, the mules laden with salt from Grange for Furness Abbey, the horses laden with copper ore from Goldscope or iron ore from the coast, and up and down that packhorse road have gone Roman, Saxon, and Dane on travellers' errands. . . .

'Up Castrigg's naked steep' we, with Wordsworth's waggoner, now make our way. But the commons enclosure has robbed it of much of its nakedness. Upon our right is seen one of the ancient milking-rings – a circular fence of holly-trees. We pass along slowly; the horses feel the hill. It is a grand view that we now have of Helvellyn, if we will but look backwards. It is hence that his majestic tawny height is best seen. It is hence that, for three parts of the year, can best be understood the meaning of his name – the Yellow Moor. . . . We are at Castle Lonning end.

To the left runs the old Penrith road to the camp or castle, to the right runs the lane to the Druid circle, unique with its thirty-eight stones in outer circle and its eastern inner sanctuary. It is a thousand pities our coach-road just misses sight of this circle. . . .

'The Moor, sir,' said the driver, and he pulled up to put the skid on.

I was right glad – the past quarter of a mile had seemed so uninteresting; it was a good preparative for a surprise.

Suddenly such a scene opened at our feet as words will not describe. Skiddaw fairly seemed to leap into the air, so suddenly did its height grow upward from the depth, that was as suddenly revealed.

Broadwater or Bassenthwaite looked as if the sea had put forth an arm of silver brightness, and was feeling its way up into the land.

Wythop and Barf and Grisedale shone mottled with wood and upland green and purple-shaded shale.

The plain was pinked and patterned out in squares of green and gold, and, like a serpent, the Derwent coiled through the fields towards the far-off lake.

There, beyond the clump of trees where nestles the vicarage of Crosthwaite, was seen the ancient parish church of good St Kentigern. Southey's resting-place was, I knew, there; and nearer, hid by the veil of trees upon its mound by Greta side, was dimly seen Greta Hall, to which at Coleridge's invitation came Robert Southey with his wife nigh heartbroken for her little one's loss in September, 1803, and from which on a dark and stormy morning, March 21, 1843, there was borne to his rest, by the side of his wife and his children three, beneath yonder white churchtower in the plain, the mortal remains of the most learned, the most unselfish, and high-minded Laureate England has known. Nearer the town is seen beneath its veil of opal smoke, St John's Church spire, and 'Derwentwater lies a queen confessed.' . . . Down the long hill we went, our skid smoking at the wheel.

And suddenly, on our left hand, Walla's Crag, Southey's favourite walk, and Falcon Crag and the Great Wood, were seen to tower up from and overhang the beautiful Lady of the Lakes, Darran or Derwentwater. There lay the burnished shield on which the wild Britons who kept their hold on Bleaberry Fell had gazed; there the calm water across which the bosom friend of great St Cuthbert, Herbert the hermit, had poured out his soul in prayer, as he paced the shore of yonder woody isle, and heard

GRASMERE, TOWNEND

Lodore
Peal to his orisons.

The glory of wonderland was ours to 'westernmost Wythop.' Now straight down the hill we go towards the little white toll-bar. The green Latrigg, on which the rude forefathers of the hamlet sleep – for forty barrows are said to have been found there in the last century – Ridge of Lathar the Dane – lies serene beneath Mount Skiddaw. Skiddaw or Skiddr the cleft one – that English model of the hornèd Parnassus, wears no cap to-day, and we rejoice, for we want fine weather; and though, when 'he shrouds his double front among Atlantic clouds, he pours forth streams more sweet than Castaly,' he at the same time hides much of the hills and sends us wet to bed.

Two ways are ours now. If the coachman takes us to the left, we shall have a magnificent peep at Borrowdale and all the reach of hills to Scawfell huge, above the Derwentwater Lake. . . .

Yes, and as we sweep down the hill by the Manor House as the house on our left with its Italian-looking tower is called, we shall get the finest view of sloping meadows and pomp of falling woods that droop toward the lake or reach upward to the sky that ever mortal gazed upon. I doubt if in the whole course of the drive there will be anything that so moves the traveller as that view southward between Walla Crag and Castlette Hill, or Castlehead, that takes the eye away over Stable Hill up to Lodore and the Gates of Borrowdale and beyond to far Scawfell. But there is always the chance of losing such a view, to suit the convenience of property owners. An application was made to divert the line of main road just here,

29

COURT HOUSES, CARLISLE

and so to send all the coaches by an easier gradient into the slack or hollow; and had it not been clearly shewn to the County Council that such a scheme would have been prejudicial to the best interests of the Keswickians, and that another good road of ascent out of the town was open to the coaches, it is likely enough the application would have been granted, to the loss of all visitors and residents for all time. . . .

But the coachman drives straight forward, and in a trice we are passing the quaint little, irregular-backed house, beneath its ash, its sycamore, its elm, and cherrytree, known as Chestnut Hill. When Shelley brought his young schoolgirl bride here in 1811, he, it is certain, did not find much more accommodation than the northern end of the roof-tree gable indicates as possible. But the garden is much as it was, in the front of the house, when he chased his young wife like a kitten round the flower-beds; and still, close by, is living the widow of the son of that old gentleman, Shelley's landlord, who was dissatisfied with the poet, thought him a dangerous occupant, found him making hydrogen sulphide gas in a retort, and bade him suit himself elsewhere.

To the right was seen just now a gate that opened to Fieldside. One cannot pass that gate without remembering that till 1890 one lived there who helped to put the laurel crown upon the poet Southey's head when he came back from London as the Laureate; one who remembered Wordsworth and Shelley; whose name is associated with the name of 'the short-lived youth,' dear to all lovers of Wordsworth, to whom the poet, then a poor and unknown man, 'owed many years of early liberty.' We have reached the bottom of the long

Chestnut Hill, and round to the left we swing. The Greta – no weeper, as some have said its name implies, to-day – is singing merrily over the pebbles hard by 'with liveliest peals of birthday harmony,' and, as one gazes back up the woody cleft wherefrom it issues, one feels that even 'to a grieved heart' such a river's 'notes' must needs be 'benisons.' Scarce seen for the woodland veil, stands Greta Bank on the cliff opposite; when that hall was but a homely farm, there, dwelt one, who, some have thought, was described by Wordsworth in the stanzas written in the pocket copy of Thomson's 'Castle of Indolence':

> Many did to him repair,
> And certes not in vain; he had inventions rare.

But, whether Calvert was 'the noticeable man with large grey eyes' thus described, or not, it is certain that there at Windy Brow lived one who loved the poets, and had more than half persuaded both Coleridge and Wordsworth to come and study chemistry with him 'within his happy castle' above the Greta banks.

'Yes, sir,' said the coachman, 'they tell that Maister Calvert, him as tried to grow corn on Latrigg, time of the famine, and as made the path to the top, lived there – fine view at Latrigg Top, sir, finest hereabouts, and it's free now for everyone, ever since the great trial they had at Carlisle, you know, sir. That's Calvert's Bridge, sir, there was such talk about, time of the trial.' Saying this, he cracked his whip, and on we went at a fine scamper past one of the most picturesque bits of solid bridge-building this side the Raise. The German miners of Queen Elizabeth's time who smelted the ore from Goldscope and Newlands in their forges close by, had only a poor wooden one here, where to-day the people go high on this solid arch of stone across to Brundholme Woods or Applethwaite. Brigham scholars are returning to their school – we are going to ours. For Keswick is here, and we have much to learn in this enchanted valley. The Fitz Park grounds are full of folk enjoying lawn-tennis and bowls. Happy little town to have such a public playground! And happy England to have such a national recreation ground as the hills and vales we have driven through today!

H.D. Rawnsley

YACHTING ON WINDERMERE

There are four of the English lakes well adapted for boat sailing, and of these Windermere is the best. The others are Coniston Water, Derwentwater, and Ullswater. Windermere is the longest with plenty of sea room at the head; between Lowwood and Wray Castle, the race-course is 18 miles long. It starts from near the Ferry, continues to Lakeside, then back past the ferry, rounding the buoy at head of lake, and finishing up at Henholme Island by Bowness Bay. The wind can be so strong on some of these lakes and the squalls so sudden that a deep boat is preferred to the skimming-dish type. The first class racer is sloop-rigged, with pole-mast, mainsail, topsail, and large jib; the bowsprit has a curious bend towards the

YACHTING ON WINDERMERE

BOWNESS BAY

water, which is thought to be better in sailing close-hauled, but would not do, of course, in a heavy sea. Roughly speaking, there are three classes of sailing-boats on Windermere – the first class racer, second class racer, and a class of una boats. There last have only been on the lake a few years, and are very serviceable: they do not draw much water, can land at most places, and having only one large mainsail are easily handled. Their hulls are a compromise between the deep and shallow type, with plenty of beam.

First class racer: length on load water-line is 22 feet, length, 32 feet; overhang forward, 4 feet; beam, 6 feet 6 inches; draft, 6 feet 6 inches; length of mast from deck to truck, 26 feet; boom, 22 feet in length; topsail yard about 18 feet; ballast 32 hundredweight, and no ballast inside yacht; deck round cockpit, 2 feet; the hoist of mainsail shall not exceed 16 feet. The second class racer is the same in rig, only a little smaller. Una boat draws 3 feet 6 inches, beam 6 feet, length 17 feet. The sail must not be too close-hauled beating against light wind, or she may get into 'irons.'

There are some curious fashions in boat-sailing on Windermere and other lakes. The main-sheet is never let to go in a squall, and luffing quickly or by degrees is only done by easing the large jib, with the tiller of course to help. In squally weather there is always a man ready at the jib-sheet. When one of the first class racers is lying well over the foot of the jib is generally in the water, and this one might suppose must retard the speed; but nobody seems to think so, and nobody minds this strange appearance, so I suppose it will go on. Then in running before the wind they never make any use of these big jibs. There is no booming out – I suppose it would be too much trouble; topsails are nearly always carried – the weather must be very bad indeed when they are not used. They sit remarkably well; I have never seen better anywhere – no jack-yards. In 'going about' these first class racers are wonderfully handy, and turn almost in their own length. There is no prettier sight than to drive down the very steep Ferry Hotel Hill, and be just in time to see thirteen or fourteen yachts manoeuvring for position three minutes before the gun fires for the start. It is rather a bird's-eye view from this hill, but one is near enough to see every detail; and, when the signal is given, what appeared before to be a crowd of white butterflies playing about in the sun, in a moment becomes orderly, straightens itself into line, and is away to the foot of the lake to round the Stott Park buoy. If one is following in a steam launch, it is time to be off: if not, there are butterflies of all hues on the ferry pier; every one is eager

32

CAMPING AT WINDERMERE

CURWEN'S ISLAND, WINDERMERE

SWAN HOTEL, NEWBY BRIDGE

and interested; there are parasols of all shades; a harp, fiddle, and piano, played exceedingly well by musicians who come every season; friends meet friends; everybody is pleased. One last look at a distant speck, which some yachtsman tells us is the *Sirius* or the *Mimosa* or the *Turtle* trying to 'steal an offing' to catch some wind off Grass Holme, and we all gradually stroll up to Ferry Hotel, where Mrs Logan, the charming hostess, may be seen for a moment straining her eyes to try to find out the leading vessel in a now quite distant fluttering little line of white.

The harpist having played his most charming passages, and the time being one o'clock, and the boats not to be back for an hour and a half, lunch is the order of the day, and we all assemble in the large dining-room of the hotel, from the windows of which there are magnificent views looking towards the head of the lake with Belle Isle or Curwen Island in the foreground. On another island close to the hotel may often be seen delightful little puppies frisking about – they are put there to be well out of mischief – the mamma swimming over from time to time to count them and see that they are all right; they belong to Mr Bruce Logan's pack of harriers.

As I have said, Windermere is best for sailing purposes, and, like most large lakes, for boat sailing has many advantages over the sea. There is no tide; there are no dangerous seas to knock a boat 'out of time'; you are never far away from land, which is made up of splendid hills covered with wood, the higher mountains showing beyond. On a rather calm day to see a group of sailing-boats, their white sails against the dark green

woods, and long reflections in the water, is a beautiful sight, which can hardly be seen anywhere to such advantage as on Windermere lake. The view from Lowwood Hotel or a little above looking toward the Langdale Pikes is one of the finest in the world; in its own way it cannot be surpassed. Then the hotels, especially Lowwood and the Ferry, are perfectly situated for boating, and the lake is quite long enough and wide enough to give plenty of variety to the sailer or even the steam launch, of which latter craft there is every kind and every speed.

Any one wishing to do a little yachting on this lake can hire, or get the right kind of boat built by some of the first-class builders, such as Brockbank or Shaw. George Brockbank has built some of the most recent and successful racers – the *Kestrel*, *Turtle*, *Mimosa*, *Mabel*, and others. Mr Shaw also has been a very successful builder.

The una boat has been found very serviceable and safe. It draws about 3 feet 6 inches; beam, 6 feet; length, 17 feet; sail area, about 270; lead, 10 hundredweight; no overhang stern allowed; 4 feet counter raking.

There is a convenient and most comfortable yacht club in Bowness Bay, about midway between the head and foot of the lake. It is the Royal Windermere Yacht Club, and was formed on the 16th of January, 1860, under the name of the 'Windermere Sailing Club.' In 1871 the headquarters were transferred to the Old England Hotel, Bowness Bay. On the 8th July 1887 Queen Victoria graciously granted permission for the use of 'Royal' to the club title. The club having

TEAL AT WATERHEAD, AMBLESIDE

increased its membership to about a hundred members, in 1889 a lease of a plot of land adjoining the grounds of the Old England Hotel, on the margin of the lake, was obtained, and a suitable club-house, containing reading-room, billiard-room, and dining-rooms, built: the use of these premises the club still enjoys.

There are also large public steamers on the lake. Some years ago there was a large private steam yacht of most graceful lines, belonging to Mr Ridehalgh, of Fellfoot; but she was too big and was inconvenient; so it was decided at last to take her off the lake.

Two boats on Windermere were designed by G.L. Watson, and one by W. Fife, jun., and Captain Sycamore of the *Shamrock* came to Windermere to see the Watson boat sail. He expressed his astonishment at all the first class sailing, and said it was the smartest he had ever seen. The Watson boat was left behind in the race.

There are plenty of yacht and boat builders at Bowness Bay, and the cost of a first class racer is about £200, all complete. July is the month for racing, but there is plenty of sailing all through the summer. The weather upon the whole is very good and well adapted for cruising. There have been some case

of accidents attended with lamentable loss of life, but never, I think, among experienced owners of boats. There are people reckless enough never to think of what may happen, or too stupid to be able to do so; to them I say, do not sail on Windermere or on any of the other English lakes in squally weather. That it can blow pretty hard on Windermere was shown a year or two ago by the sinking of one of the large iron steamers at her moorings near the foot of the lake. It is supposed that the lake rose very quickly, and, her mooring chain being rather short, the waves began to break over her until she sank where she was in quite a narrow part of the lake.

I was glad to see the other day at Euston Station some capital views of Windermere and photographs of yachts sailing; one a very good picture of two vessels lying well over to a strong puff of wind. This gives a very good idea of the kind of thing. Any of my readers inclined to take to sailing had better go and have a look at these admirable photographs. If they approve, the booking-office is close at hand, and nothing is easier than to order a luncheon-basket to be put in at Stafford and to buy a ticket for Windermere.

Arthur Severn

35

HOLKER HALL, CARTMEL

THE SKULLS OF CALGARTH

A Legend of Windermere Lake

This old mansion of Calgarth, on the banks of Lake Windermere, is built much in the style of Levens and Sizergh. Some of the rooms have been elegantly finished; but, having been a long time in the possession of farmers, who occupy but a part of it, it is much gone out of repair, and has, on the whole, a melancholy appearance. This circumstance, in concurrence with the superstitious notions which have ever been common in country places, and the particular mentioned hereafter, have probably given rise to a report, which has long prevailed, that the house is haunted. And many are the stories of frightful visions and mischievous deeds which the goblins of the place are said to have performed, to terrify and distress the harmless neighbourhood. These fables are not yet entirely disbelieved. Spectres still are seen, and there are two human skulls, which have lain in the window of a large room as long as can be remembered, whose history and reputed properties are too singular not to contribute something to this story of 'the haunted house,' and to let them be passed over in this route.

It has been a popular tale in these parts of immemorial standing, that these skulls formerly belonged to two poor old people, who were unjustly executed for a robbery; to perpetuate their innocence, some ghost brought them there; and that they are, for that end, indestructible, and in effect, 'immoveable.' For, it is said, to what place soever they were taken, or however used, they were still presently seen again in their old dormitory, the window. As the report goes, they have been buried, burned, powdered, and dispersed in the winds, and upon the lake, several times, to no purpose as to their removal and destruction: so far, say common fame. Certain it is these human remains still exist, and it would be thought an impeachment of the taste and curiosity of the nymphs and swains of the neighbouring villages, if they could not say they had once seen the skulls of Calgarth.

As a more rational account of the matter (though still lame and unsatisfactory), it is told by some, that there formerly lived in the house a famous doctress, who had two skeletons by her, for the usual purposes of her profession; and the skulls happening to meet with better preservation than the rest of the bones, they were accidentally honoured with this singular notice. But, be their origin what it may, their legend is too whimsical and improbable to deserve being recorded, otherwise than as an instance of the never-failing credulity of ignorance and superstition.

Wilson Armistead

ROSE COTTAGE, SEATHWAITE, DUNNERDALE

HEAVY RAINFALL

Rain, we are afraid, is generally looked on as the plague of the English lakes – and not without some justification as will be seen from the following comparative statistics which we have extracted from a table printed by Mr F.C. Bayard, F.R. Met. Soc., in the Society's Quarterly Journal. We have selected for the purpose of rough comparison the mean rainfall between 1881–1890 at Seathwaite, in Borrowdale (the wettest village in the whole district), and at Brighton, Scarborough, Lowestoft, and Ilfracombe, as broadly representative of South, North, East, and West. The result is certainly startling!

Seathwaite	Scarborough	Lowestoft	Brighton	Ilfracombe
129.04	27.50	24.16	28.75	30.63

Seathwaite, of course, is an extreme example; and, lest prospective visitors should be discouraged, we append a second table of the mean rainfall at a number of different places in the district itself. The figures are taken from Mr Symons' *British Rainfall* for 1897. The average, however, are in this case calculated over different periods of years.

	Limiting Dates	Computed Mean Rainfall
Coniston	1865–76	76.5
Keswick	1864–69	55.7
Bowness	1871–80	58.5
Ullswater (Hallsteads)	1845–86	53.2
Buttermere	1887–96	107.2
Wythburn	1878–90	89.5
Grasmere (High Close)	1858–96	80.6

These figures, it will be seen, though less formidable than those for Seathwaite – where it once rained 8.03 inches in a single day (November 12, 1897)! – tell practically the same tale. If, however, we compare the Lakes with other *hill* districts in England, the difference is no longer quite so alarming, though still sufficiently great. This time we have chosen for comparison the wettest recorded places for a single year in the mountainous parts of Carnarvon, Merioneth, Brecknock, Yorkshire, Derbyshire, and Devon. The figures are again from Mr Symons' *British Rainfall* for 1897.

Carnarvon (Llanbedr-y-Cennin)	Merioneth (Blaenau Ffestiniog)	Brecknock (Taff Fechan)
82.77	115.82	101.54
Yorkshire (Slaidburn)	Devon (Prince Town)	Derbyshire (Buxton)
78.98	81.93	51.23
Cumberland (The Stye)	Westmorland (Mickleden)	Lancashire (Coniston)
197.39	137.63	101.58

THE GRASMERE PIER

Cumberland and Westmorland, it will be seen from this table, still retain their bad pre-eminence!

There still remains the important question – which is the wettest month? The following mean rainfalls from 1881–97 are taken from Mr Symons' *British Rainfall*.

Jan.	Feb.	Mar.	April.	May.	June.
12.25	11.20	11.38	6.04	7.32	6.52

July.	Aug.	Sept.	Oct.	Nov.	Dec.
9.98	11.63	12.58	12.04	14.07	15.05

In the face of these figures it can scarcely be denied that the district is exceptionally rainy, but it is well to remember that to this very fact it owes a great deal of its charm. We remember walking up from Mardale Head to Small Water after a previous day of almost incessant rain, and shall not easily forget the beauty of the innumerable copious cataracts leaping in all directions down the sides of the fells. On another occasion we visited the Lake country at the beginning of the break-up of a six weeks drought, and the parched hill slopes and dried up becks had robbed the district of a large part of its charm. Half the beauty and all the music of the fells are dependent on the existence of excessive wet weather.

Pearson's Gossipy Guide to the English Lakes

SEATHWAITE, DUNNERDALE

GRANGE-IN-BORROWDALE

BORROWDALE

We are now traversing scenery which, for mingled grandeur and loveliness, is, perhaps, unsurpassed in the Kingdom. Kit North has declared, in a burst of confidence, that he had traversed every glen of the Scottish Highlands, but was sorrowfully compelled to admit that Borrowdale remained without rival! On either side the craggy and fantastic mountains descend immediately to the copious river, whose clear green waters surge majestically on their pebbly bed. Their lower slopes are variegated with heather, and feathered with silver birch. In the distance, up the valley, are the peaks of Glaramara, and the culminating summits of Scafell Pike and Great End. No space is left for a single green field, or for human habitation. Nature here, with the exception of the road, reigns in undisputed possession.

This, we suppose, was probably the point where the Borrowdale men formerly built their celebrated wall which was to ensure them perpetual spring, by imprisoning and retaining the cuckoo. Spring and the cuckoo, these philosophers had noted, invariably arrived together, and together the two departed. What more natural than to connect the two as cause and effect, and to attribute the grateful influence of the season to the presence in the valley of the cuckoo? The problem had now become simple – let them prevent the migration of the bird, and the spring would become perpetual. With this end in view they began to build a wall across the bottom of the valley, but as they still worked at it with feverish hast, the ominous 'cuckoo' was heard coming down the dale as the bird made its way from tree to tree. At last the cricital moment arrived, and the visitor came to the barrier. Was it already high enough? Alas! the cuckoo skimmed quietly over it, but only a foot or two above its summit! The angry despair of baffled Borrowdale is better imagined than described; for had the wall only risen a few courses higher, the bird would have been their prisoner! The story has been told by Miss Martineau. It would seem, indeed, that 'Borrowdale Gowks,' like 'Austwick Carles' in Yorkshire, formerly enjoyed an extended reputation for their feather-headed wits. As we feel sure that the reputation is undeserved to-day, we have less hesitation in recording it.

Pearson's Gossipy Guide to the English Lakes

ULLSWATER, PATTERDALE

ULLSWATER

Perhaps it will be of interest to add a list of Royal and other personages who have visited Patterdale during the past half century. In 1840, the Dowager Queen Adelaide and her sister Ida, Duchess of Saxe Weimar, with a numerous suite, stayed at Patterdale; and in the same year two foreign princes from Ashantee stayed here. In 1844, the King of Saxony and suite visited Patterdale. In August of the same year Prince William of Prussia stayed here. In 1857, his Royal Highness the Prince of Wales arrived at Keswick, and on the Sunday attended divine service in the church at Patterdale. In August, 1895, H.I.M. William II., Emperor of Germany, and suite made a tour right through the district, the steam yacht 'Raven' being especially commissioned by the Earl of Lonsdale to convey his august guest from Pooley to Patterdale. The Duke of Cambridge and other English and foreign notabilities have of recent years made visits to Patterdale.

The Official Guide of the Ullswater Steam Navigation Co. Ltd

THE ROYAL MAIL STEAM YACHTS

Of the Ullswater Steam Navigation Co., Ltd., will ply (weather permitting and Sundays excepted) on the Lake from Easter to the beginning of October:

STEAMBOAT FARES

	SINGLE		RETURN	
Between	1st Cl.	2nd Cl.	1st Cl.	2nd Cl.
	s. d.	s. d.	s. d.	s. d.
Pooley Bridge and Howtown	1 0	0 9	1 6	1 3
Howtown and Patterdale	1 6	1 0	2 0	1 6
Pooley Bridge and Patterdale	2 0	1 6	3 0	2 0

COACH FARES

Between Penrith and Pooley Bridge: Single, 2s. 0d.; Return, 2s. 6d. (Coachman's Fee included.) Children under 12 half-price.

RETURN TICKETS

Return Tickets are available for day of issue only, except those issued on Saturdays which are available for return on Mondays.

KING STREET, PENRITH

PLEASURE PARTIES, &c.

Pleasure Parties of not less than Ten will be taken at Half Return Fare for the Double Journey on one day's notice being given to the Secretary or Captain, except by Boats leaving Patterdale at 1.40 and Pooley Bridge at 2.55 p.m.

Season Tickets £1; Monthly Tickets, 15s. each.
Weekly Tickets, 1st Class 6/6, 2nd Class 4/6.
Dogs 3d. each. Bicycles, &c., 6d. each.

COACHES FOR ULLSWATER

Leave the chief Hotels in Bowness (Windermere) about 9.20 a.m., and the 'Windermere Hotel,' the 'Hydropathic,' &c., Windermere, twenty minutes later, arriving at Kirkstone Pass at 11.30 a.m. and Ullswater at 12.40 p.m. ·Fares: Single, 6/-; Return, 8/6.

Coaches leave the 'Waterhead,' Ambleside, about 9.30 a.m.; and the 'Salutation' and chief Hotels in Ambleside at 10.0 a.m., arriving at Kirkstone Pass at 11.0 a.m. and Ullswater at 12.15 p.m. ·Fares: Single, 3/6 and 4/-; Return, 5/-.

Coaches also leave Troutbeck (for Ullswater) at 10.30 a.m., reaching Patterdale at 11.30 a.m. Fares: Single, 3/6; Return, 5/-.

·Previous to Whitsuntide the fares from Bowness, Windermere, and Ambleside, are subject to there being three or more passengers. The above-named Coaches wait the arrival of 3.40 boat at Patterdale. Coaches for Ambleside leave

PORTER AND COACHMAN, THE COUNTY HOTEL, AMBLESIDE

CHURCH WALK, ALLITHWAITE

Patterdale at 10.30 a.m. and 2.0 p.m., when three or more passengers only, returning in time for boat about 7.20 p.m. Fares: Single 5/–; Return, 6/6.

Coaches leave Patterdale for Troutbeck at 8.20 a.m. and 4.0 p.m.

The Official Guide of the Ullswater Steam Navigation Co. Ltd

THE LAKE DISTRICT DEFENCE SOCIETY

Those interested in preserving the scenery of our English Lakes in its natural beauty should become members of the Lake District Defence Society. Secretary and Treasurer, G. SOMERVELL, Esq., Hazelthwaite, Windermere.

Those interested in preserving the footpaths of the Kendal and Windermere neighbourhood, should communicate with E. WHITWELL, Esq., Secretary, Footpath Society, Kendal.

Those who meet with obstruction to ancient rights of way in the Keswick neighbourhood, should write to T. PAULIN, Esq., The Beeches, Keswick.

It is especially requested–

(1) That tourists will not take dogs on to the fells or through the woods, unless under complete control: they disturb both sheep and game.

(2) That they will not root up ferns and flowers, nor break down boughs of trees in blossom time. Ferns can be procured of local nurserymen, and all varieties are best propagated from seed. The Lake District is fast losing its attractive flora by reason of this foolish robbery.

(3) That gates from pasture to pasture be closed carefully after having passed through them.

(4) That walls shall not be broken down in crossing the high fells.

(5) That pedestrians, where a beaten track exists, will keep to it and not trespass, but will determinedly remove, after due enquiry, any recent obstruction to an ancient well-defined pathway.

(6) That picnic parties will not leave about broken bottles, egg shells, or paper.

(7) That, so far as in them lies, they will see that the horses they drive are kindly entreated. Gentlemen can always walk up the steeper hills. And everyone can help to secure both horses and drivers a very necessary rest by refusing to hire carriages on Sunday.

H.D. Rawnsley

MARYPORT AND CARLISLE ENGINE AT CURROCK SHED, CARLISLE

MARYPORT: COMMERCE, ETC.

Ships were first registered at Maryport in 1838, in which year the Custom House and the Old Harbour office in Strand Street were built. The former of these is now used for offices by Messrs Hine, Bros., Shipping Agents, whilst the latter has been superseded by the Town Hall, in Senhouse Street, built in 1890.

On February 3rd, 1842, the Port was entirely separated from Whitehaven, to which it had been previously subsidiary. In the same year the Bonded Warehouse in Lower Church Street was built. In 1898, the new Custom House in Curzon Street, was built, and the port is now the chief Customs port on the coast.

The Maryport and Carlisle Railway had proved no inconsiderable factor in producing those changes which have been for the welfare of Maryport. Incorporated by Act of Parliament, 1 Victoria c. 3 (1837), from Maryport to Aspatria was opened July 15th, 1840. The first engine, the 'Ellen,' was floated to Maryport on a raft from Lowca. From Carlisle to Wigton was opened in May, 1844, the whole line being opened May 10th, 1845. Mr George Stephenson was the consulting engineer. It was originally proposed that the line should be called the 'Carlisle and Whitehaven Railway Co.,'

but this was not entertained. However, an extension to Whitehaven was not long delayed, that portion of the line being opened March 18th, 1847. In 1855, an Act was obtained granting power to double the line between Maryport and Carlisle.

New energy was now infused into the harbour works. In 1846 the lighthouse, now superseded, was erected, and, in the following year, the harbour was greatly improved, the wooden pier being extended after the memorable storm of December 26th, 1852. During this period the harbour revenue was as follows:

	£	s.	d.		£	s.	d.
1834	1,654	17	10 ½	1851	3,858	8	5
1837	1,800	0	0	1854	6,094	13	8

Such an increase necessitated further extensions, and hence, after some preliminary work, it was decided to build what is now the Elizabeth Dock. Begun in 1854, it was opened October 20th, 1857, amidst great rejoicings. Its length is 600 feet, and breadth 240 feet, enclosing an area of nearly 3½ acres. The engineer was Mr Dees, and the contractor, Mr Nelson, of Carlisle. The depth of water on the sill at ordinary spring tides is 20 feet, and at neap tides, 14 feet. In 1865 a

SILLOTH HARBOUR

further attempt at extension was made, Mr Page, C.E., making a report 'on the proposed Harbour of Refuge, New Basin, and Dock.' The north side was favoured, but the project came to nothing. The revenue however, kept on increasing by leaps and bounds, as follows:

	£	s.	d.		£	s.	d.
1857	6,636	5	4	1879	8,900	0	0
1869	6,760	0	0	1881	10,641	11	11
1870	6,407	0	0	1882	12,969	11	0
1874	6,308	2	10	1883	11,850	18	4

The Elizabeth Dock, of course, was not calculated to cope with this rapidly increasing trade, nor was it suited for the larger class of boats which now came to the port. Hence, a larger dock, with accommodation for large ocean going ships, was determined on. Two sites were named, the one on the north, and the other on the south side of the river mouth. Eventually the south side was determined upon, and the first sod was cut by Mrs Senhouse on February 26th, 1880. The engineers were Sir John Hawkshaw, Son, and Hayter, the contractor being Mr W.J. Doherty, of Dublin. The work was greatly delayed through the damage done by the great storms

of November 23rd and 27th, 1881, when the works were flooded, and the embankment carried away. To provide against future contingencies of a like nature, it became necessary to very materially alter the plans, thus involving a very much larger expenditure than had been originally intended. However, in due course, the new dock was completed and named the Senhouse Dock. It was opened by Mrs Senhouse on May 27th, 1884. The day was observed as a general holiday, a commemorative medal being issued on the occasion. It may be worthy of remark that the first vessel to enter the dock was the ss *Alne Holme*, owned by the Messrs Hine Bros. The length of the dock is 850 feet, and its breadth 300 feet, hence it has an area of nearly 6 acres. The depth of water on the sill at ordinary spring tides is 25 feet, and at neap tides 19 feet.

That the promoters were fully justified in the erection of this new dock is clear when we consider the large increase that has taken place in the revenue since 1883. Thus:

1884	£ 9,520	1891	£18,000	1899	£26,000
1885	£12,269	1894	£17,000	1900	£34,600
1886	£19,088	1897	£27,000	1901	£31,800
1888	£24,000	1898	£28,000		

BRAYTON COLLIERY COAL PICKERS

As showing the capacity of the Dock, it is worthy of remark that in 1886 the two largest vessels leaving carried 3,793 and 3,802 tons respectively, whilst in 1898 the largest was 5,000 tons. From 1755–1867 the export of coal was as follows:

	Tons			Tons
1755–1781	765,530		1853	269,000
1828	40,000		1854	300,504
1839	101,104		1857	341,068
1841	150,000		1867	476,162

From 1868 forward the Chief Imports were:

	Iron Ore Tons	Timber Tons	General Merchandise Tons	Anthracite Coal Tons
1868	656	–	–	–
1869	–	–	–	–
1870	1,270	–	2,983	–
1885	47,164	9,730	22,319	–
1886	86,178	5,481	22,751	–
1888	144,615	4,891	25,053	14,456
1891	71,309	4,762	24,584	1,290
1894	69,319	5,143	22,181	3,150
1896	187,000	3,300	25,000	–

During the same period the chief Exports have been:

	Coal Tons	Pig Iron Tons	Steel Rails Tons
1868	406,718	263,428	–
1869	420,604	270,002	–
1870	454,604	287,943	–
1877	297,903	–	–
1882	212,931	–	–
1885	196,201	80,546	6,791
1886	208,990	72,698	75,957
1888	189,675	50,936	61,711
1891	177,117	82,772	93,935
1894	245,050	15,482	90,627
1896	200,000	Nil	150,000

In addition, also, Stone, Lime, Bar, Bolt, and Cast Iron, and General Merchandise were amongst the exports.

The total amount of the imports and exports during this period was:

	Imports Tons	Exports Tons
1885	89,313	285,399
1886	126,752	360,084
1888	189,015	305,187
1891	101,945	358,516
1894	99,793	352,986
1896	215,300	352,500
1897	406,000	305,000
1898	385,000	373,000

SLATE QUARRY, KIRKBY-IN-FURNESS

The total money value of the Dock Works in 1899 was £314,696, the various Bonds being in five classes, the respective holdings being: 1, £54,155; 2, £1,950; 3, £125,870; 4, £84,600; 5, £48,121.

A few words are necessary with regard to the manufactures of Maryport, past and present.

The manufacture of *glass* was carried on behind the offices of Messrs Hine Bros., shipbrokers; that of *salt*, at Saltpans; of *cotton*, in what is now Messrs Carr's Flour Mill; of *paper*, at Paper Mill Green; and of *lead pencils*, at Ellengrove. All these are now of the past.

A few remarks are, however, necessary with regard to *iron*, the oldest of the manufactures of Maryport. A company was formed, and a lease granted in 1752 for a term of 50 years of land in close proximity to Mote Hill. The said lease was 'granted to James Postlethwaite, of Cartmel; William Lewthwaite, of Kirkby Hall; William Postlethwaite, of Kirkby; Thomas Hartley, John Gale, Edward Tubman, and Edmund Gibson, all of Whitehaven; of buildings, quarries, and land on which to erect furnaces and forges, with power to deepen the river Ellen between the works and the harbour. . . . The works, in 1784, comprised a blast furnace some 36 feet high, or, to the top of the chimney, of 43 feet. It stands on a base 30 feet square. . . . The present inside diameter of the bottom is 8 feet; and at 7 feet from the bottom, the diameter at the bosh is 12 feet 6 inch.' There were besides 'three large coal houses, which will contain charcoal or coke sufficient for a year's blast; three commodious houses for the storing of iron ores; three dwelling-houses for workmen; a large and convenient casting

CARTMEL SQUARE

BRAYTON COLLIERY YARD

house, with a very good furnace, by which the foundry branch may be carried on to the greatest extent; seventeen ovens for charring coals, built on an improved plan, and which make a cinder superior to any other method; and a neat well-built dwelling-house, most agreeably situated, and very convenient for the works.' Such was the inventory. The iron ore for use at this furnace is stated to have been brought across Broughton Moor on pack horses, whilst, in 1781, small quantities were imported from Whitehaven and Ulverstone, and returned to those places as pig iron; whilst a quantity was brought from Palnackie, Kirkcudbright, in a very small vessel, which discharged its cargo close to the works. About 1863, a 'pig,' made here, was found with the initials H.S. and the date 1769; whilst in May, 1895, two others were found, one of which was dated 1755. All are now preserved at Netherhall. The work 'was occasionally stopped for want of water to turn the wheel which worked the blast cylinders indeed, the ultimate failure of the enterprise was doubtless occasioned by this uncertainty of the water supply.' At any rate in November, 1783, Mr John Barnes, in a letter to Mr Senhouse, said it was the wish of the Furnace Company to sell the lease on account of the embarrassed state of the concern. The final settlement was made in January, 1784, Mr Senhouse taking over the

concern at a valuation. It is not very clear whether the work was continued after this date.

The Maryport Haematite Iron Co., formed in 1868, had six furnaces, but suspended work in 1882. The Solway Iron Co, formed in 1870, had four furnaces, but suspended work in 1894. Messrs Cammell's, however, took up the work in the latter yard, and at present (1899) are doing a brisk business in pig iron, etc. There seems to be a prospect of a great revival of the iron trade in this district at no distant date.

Shipbuilding, some years ago, gave employment to a large number of hands, and the shipyards of Wood, Ritson, Peat & Middleton, turned out a great number of wood-built ships of a superior class. Three of these yards are now closed. Messrs Ritson, however, introduced the making of a large class of iron ships, and are now (1899) making arrangments for a large extension of their business. Most of their ships are launched on the almost unique broadside plan.

Flour, iron founding, sail making, tanning and brewing occupy a fair share of attention. Messrs Carr have lately rebuilt, and largely extended their premises, – the old cotton factory, – whilst the same remark applies to the tannery, which has been carried on so successfully by Messrs Williamson for so many years.

CHARCOAL BURNING, NEAR HAVERTHWAITE

Maryport was first supplied with gas in 1834 by a private company. In 1866, however, the Trustees acquired the power to make gas for the harbour and streets, the older company continuing to supply the houses. Such a dual control could not exist. Negotiations were entered upon, but it was not till 1876 that the Trustees bought out the old company, and now supply the whole of the gas required. During 1882, the production of gas was 16,500,000 cubic feet; whilst in 1898, it amounted to 30,386,000 cubic feet.

Maryport is a station for the Royal Naval Reserve. A new battery was built in one corner of the field in which is the Roman Camp in 1886.

The Mechanics' Institute, founded in 1842, was originally held in a house in Crosby Street, but was transferred to its present home in the Athenaeum in 1856. There are now (1899) 259 members, and there are some 2,000 books in the library.

The population has increased steadily, as is shown by the following table:

1774–1,300	1851– 5,698
1801–2,932	1861– 6,037
1811–3,134	1871– 7,137
1821–3,514	1881– 8,126

1831–3,877	1891–12,536
1841–5,311	

Bulmers History & Directory of Cumberland, 1901

BACKBARROW IRON WORKS, NEAR HAVERTHWAITE

These now consist of one Charcoal Iron Furnace, and are built entirely of stone, and bear the date of 1710. It is the last of five at one time worked by Messrs Harrison, Ainslie and Company (the others being at Bonawe, Argyleshire; Duddon Bridge, Cumberland; Warsash, Southampton; and Newland, near Ulverston), and is the only furnace in this country that produces charcoal pig-iron. The fuel is obtained from the woods in the neighbourhood. The blast is cold, and is blown by water-power from the River Leven upon which the works are situated. The production is from 30 to 35 tons per week, but the furnace is at present out, and will not be put into blast until the end of August 1901.

Institute of Mechanical Engineers Proceedings, July 1901

BASSENTHWAITE ROAD, KESWICK

PROPOSED WRYNOSE–HARDKNOTT ROAD

Mr Little said that in the year 1881 a scheme for a road across Hardknott was proposed, though in a cruder form, and was before the Association at that time. The Association since then had at various times given grants for the repair of the existing road. Thirty years ago it was proposed to improve the road, at a cost of something like £2,000, but the proposal fell through for lack of support. Now they had come to a larger scheme, prepared by a member of the Association.

The Scheme Explained

The exponent of the scheme, with the aid of several plans and maps, then gave an explanation of the undertaking. He said: Your secretary has invited me here to explain my scheme for a reconstruction of the old road over the Wrynose and Hardknott Passes. I begin by pointing out that a good carriage-road from East to West is the greatest need of the Lake District, for both tourists and local residents. Most of the traffic enters the district through Windermere village, and we have an excellent road running north through Ambleside to Thirlmere, Keswick, and Bassenthwaite Lake. A good road also runs north-eastward over Kirkstone Pass to Ullswater and Penrith. To the west, the district from Grasmere and the Langdales southward between Consiton and Windermere

SANTON BRIDGE

LONGTOWN ROADMEN, *c.* 1910

Lakes is well supplied with roads, but the only feasible carriage road to Wastwater, Eskdale, and the western coast involves a long detour by Broughton-in-Furness and Millom. Keswick, the other great centre in the Lake District, is well supplied with roads – from Penrith and Ullswater on the east, from Ambleside and Thirlmere on the south, and from Bassenthwaite, Buttermere, Crummock Water, Ennerdale Lake, etc., on the west. A great mountain wall extends from Keswick in the north to Millom in the south, a distance in a straight line of 28 miles. This line passes through Scafell Pike; and exactly midway this wall is broken by the Hardknott Pass, which forms a continuation of the Wrynose Gap. North of this the only carriage-road crosses at Honister Pass, but this is useless as a through route, as the map shows. South of Hardknott there are indeed roads across Birker Moor at Ulpha and over Stoneside Hill to Bootle, but both are very rough and steep, and involve nearly as a long a detour (to Broughton) as the main coast road by Millom. The one and only obvious gap in this range is the Wrynose–Hardknott Passes, which are both only 1,250 feet high, which is 250 feet lower than Kirkstone Pass, and only about 50 feet higher than Honister Pass. The Romans saw the strategic importance of this gap, and made one of their famous roads across it from their camp at Ambleside to their port at Ravenglass, with a camp midway at Hardknott. Since their time very little improvement has been

RAVENGLASS

BUILDING SHOPFORD BRIDGE AT THE LIMEKILN INN, BEWCASTLE

made on this road, and although till the introduction of railways it remained an important pack-horse track, the existing road is little more than a cart-road, hardly fit for carriages, very rough, very steep (one in five in places), and with most dangerous turns.

I have compiled a table of comparative distances to places on the western side of the Lake District from Ambleside, Kendal, and Lancaster respectively, by Broughton, by Keswick, and by the new road. This shows very considerable reductions, e.g., Ambleside to Wasdale Head is reduced from 46 miles by Broughton, and 52 by Keswick to 26 by Wrynose; to Seascale, 40 miles, 44, and 24 respectively. A new coaching tour from Ambleside could be opened if this new road were made. Instead of merely 'the round of the Langdales,' coaches could run from Ambleside to the Stanley Ghyll Hotel at Boot in Eskdale, whence, after lunch, tourists could proceed in fresh coaches to Wastdale Head, approaching it in the best way from a scenic point of view, viz., up the lake, with the glorious view of the Wastwater Screes. Eskdale, too, is a very little known district which would rapidly develop with proper access, possessing as it does charming wooded and river scenery, the finest waterfall in the district, Stanley Ghyll, and the finest Roman remains – Hardknott camp, with its magnificent view of the Scafell range and of the Irish Sea, with the Isle of Man in the distance. Duddon-dale also would be rendered much more accessible by the branch road improvement, one and a quarter mile long from Cockley

Beck, instead of by the present round-about route by Broughton. This valley also is far too little known and possesses most beautiful scenery of all kinds. Local residents would benefit by much shorter distances between the farms and villages, and by the far greater traffic and rapid development which would follow improved communications.

I have shown, on the plan and section exhibited, the alterations which I consider necessary to make a useful twelve-foot through road with gradients not steeper than one in ten and curves of not less than two chains radius. The levels are taken from the six-inch ordnance map, and so are approximate only in places near the summits of the passes; but they are sufficiently accurate for preliminary purposes. I show a table giving the lengths of the various works in yards and an estimate of the probable outside cost, adopting for this purpose the prices of 37s. 6d. per lineal yard for deviations and 8s. per lineal yard for improvements where the old line and level are kept practically the same. You will notice that the costs of the various works are allotted between the three counties of Westmorland, Cumberland, and Lancashire – for the old and new roads both lie partly in all three counties, so that the cost would be shared. The total length of deviations necessary is 9,670 yards, or five and a half miles, and of improvements on the main route 2,880 yards, or one and five-eighth miles. The Duddon Valley branch improvement is 2,270 yards, or one and a quarter miles. Total, 14,820 yards, or eight and three-eighth miles. Particulars of my estimates per lineal yard are given on

KEEKLE TERRACE, CLEATOR

the section; these include special works such as bridges. The total costs to each county work out as follows: Cumberland, £9,955; Lancashire, £4,867; Westmorland, £5,369; total, £20,191. This should not be excessive in view of the assistance which would probably be given by the Road Board. The costs may seem to you too low or too high; if so, all you have to do is to take the lengths given and work out the costs at a fresh price per lineal yard. The proportions would in any case remain the same, viz., Cumberland would pay half, and Lancashire and Westmorland one-fourth each approximately. And this is right, for Cumberland is far larger, more populous, and wealthier than Westmorland, while Lancashire benefits least by the scheme, and that chiefly owing to the Lake District being the 'play-ground' for Lancashire's millions. Then, too, Cumberland would benefit most by the opening up of its south-western district, which is now even declining owing to the closing of the railway from Ravenglass to Boot and of the Stanely Ghyll Hotel.

English Lake District Association

ROADS

Steam rollers were first used in Westmorland for repairing the main roads in 1886. They were 10 tons in weight – smaller ones were afterwards used on the secondary roads, and the larger ones with scarifier attachments were introduced in 1903.

For the year ending March 31st, 1890, the cost of the upkeep of the main roads to the County Council was:

Repairs and Improvements of Main Roads	£5075	7	7
Main Roads maintained by Urban Authorities	1677	2	4
Contribution towards Cost of Public Highways, Sec. 11, Sub.-Sec. 10, Act of 1888	290	9	8
Total cost	£7042	19	7

The cost of the upkeep of the main roads for the year ending 31st March, 1900, had risen to:

Repair and Improvement of Main Roads	£7600	2	6
Ditto, repaired by Urban Authorities	3237	17	2
Contribution towards Cost of Public Highways, Sec. 11, Sub-Sec. 10, Act of 1888	537	0	0
Total cost	£11374	19	8

F. W. Garnett

KIRKBY LONSDALE DEVIL'S BRIDGE

Near to the bridge which crosses the Lune, not far from Kirkby Lonsdale, the scenery is truly romantic. The river, which is here of considerable width, winds through the bottom of the valley, and is overshadowed by the trees that grow upon its banks. Its current is roughened by the rocks which form its bed, some of which stand up in huge moss-grown blocks in the midst of the stream. The water is clear to a great depth, and the steep grassy banks, and abundance of trees which close in the prospect, give it an air of seclusion. This stream is plentifully stocked with trout and salmon, and here the angler may sit and watch the gilded fly with a devotion worthy of a Davy or a Walton.

The singular construction of the bridge renders it an object of curiosity; and when viewed in connection with the river and valley of the Lune, it forms one of the most romantic prospects on which the eye can dwell. It is composed of three beautifully ribbed arches, the centre one rising to the height of thirty-six feet above the stream. It is a lofty, firm and handsome structure, but so narrow as almost to deserve the taunt cast upon the 'auld brig of Ayr:'

Where twa wheelbarrows trembled when they met:

at least no two carriages of a larger size can pass each other; but, for the security of the foot passengers, there are angular recesses in the battlements, corresponding with the projecting piers.

Antiquity has cast her veil over this erection, and a consequent obscurity envelopes its history. If, however, we

KIRKBY LONSDALE SQUARE

HESKET SHOW, 1905

may rely on popular tradition, the building is to be ascribed to an unmentionable personage; of whom it is said, 'that he built the bridge one windy night, and that in fetching the stones from a distance, he let fall the last apronfull as he flew over a fell hard by.' This gentleman has been 'a bridge-builder,' 'time out of mind,' notwithstanding the improbability of his employing 'himself in works of so much real utility to men.' Such an historical fact may, however, account for the huge blocks of stone found in various parts of the neighbouring moors.

Wilson Armistead

HORSES

C.W. Wilson, of Oxenholme, now of Rigmaden, had done more than any other single individual to develop horse-breeding in the county, starting, as he did, in the early seventies. At his sale in September, 1880, he had catalogued 11 Clydesdale mares and stallions, 53 Hackneys, 2 Coach stallions, and 7 Roadster stallions, including 'Lord Derby' and 'Star of the Garter'; he was placed first with the former at the Paris Exhibition in 1878, and in the following year, when the Royal was at Kilburn, was placed first for his Cleveland stallion

'Penzance' for getting coach horses, and also took the principal prizes both for mares and stallions in the pony classes; indeed, for some years he dominated at all the shows in these classes, and his famous sire, 'Sir George,' will never be forgotten. To establish his breed, Wilson selected the best Fell ponies (mares) of the hill districts and crossed them with Sir George, and turned the produce out on the fells and moors round Rigmaden to fend for themselves; his ponies became eligible for the Hackney Stud Book.

The Hackney Stud Book was first published in 1884, according to which 'Wroots Pretender' was the first Hackney in the county coming to Kirkby Stephen from Long Sutton in Lincolnshire, being brought by a *break-neck-dealer* from Yorkshire. Although there was a class for Hackneys at the Kendal Show in 1868, it was not till 1880 that the Society included them in their Spring Stallion Show as 'Horses for getting Hackneys,' but there were still only two classes in 1885 at their annual show – Thoroughbreds and Cart stallions. In the following year, although there was no class, Abbott, of Kirkby Lonsdale, exhibited his Hackney stallion 'Lord Chancellor,' and in 1889 C.W. Wilson showed 'Lord Walton' and 'Sunbeam.' In 1891 the classes at the Kendal Spring Show were for Thoroughbreds with two entries and Cart stallions with five, but there were also paraded on the ground a Cleveland bay, two Hackneys, and a Roadster. The premiums

KENDAL HORSE FAIR

offered continued to be a silver medal in the two classes, till 1906, since when the Kendal Agriculture Society has merely arranged a parade on an advertised Saturday afternoon. In 1910 the parade was held in Longlands on the 16th of April, when 4 Thoroughbred, 6 Hackney, 7 Shire, 3 Clydesdale, and 1 Pony stallion were on view.

In 1887 the Royal Agricultural Society inaugurated their Thoroughbred Stallion Show at Newcastle, offering five premiums of £200 for sires to serve 50 approved mares at £2 10s. each, one of the winners, 'Moss Hawk,' was allotted to Westmorland. 'Moss Hawk' was described by Wm. Blew as 'a nicely topped horse, and his fine forehead was much admired . . . when he paraded round the ring his bloodlike appearance was all the more apparent. If there is a fault to be found with him it is in his hocks, but the shortcomings did not seem to be very serious. . . . he brings no character with him from the racecourse.' In the following year, in conjunction with the Hunters' Improvement Society and the Royal Commission on Horse Breeding, the scheme was greatly extended, and a premium thoroughbred has usually been allotted to the district ever since. In 1893–4 and 5 Dr Iliffe, of Kendal, won one of these premiums with 'Button Park.'

The Royal Commission on Horse Breeding terminated in 1911, the Board of Agriculture taking up the supply of thoroughbred sires through the development grant.

John Singleton, who rode the winner of the first great St Leger in 1776 and jockeyed 'Eclipse' in all his great races, was born at Kendal in 1736. He died in his 90th year at Chester House of Industry.

F.W. Garnett

FELLGATE, WOODLAND

SHEARING AT MANSRIGGS, ULVERSTON

SHEEP

A peculiarity of the Herdwicks is their fondness for the heaf upon which they have been bred and accustomed to pasture; so great is this love or homing instinct that special covenants are inserted in all leases relating to the letting of Herdwicks. No obstacle is too great to prevent a Herdwick, which has been sold and removed a dozen or more miles away, returning to its native heaf – they are sad home-wanderers, as many farmers know who have bought them for crossing or winter feeding. Many an old wether is retained on account of his usefulness in 'keeping the heaf,' even when his teeth are gone, not only does he keep strangers off, but he educates the young sheep of the flock till they are accustomed to their heaf.

The tups are loosed about Martinmas till the middle or even latter end of December, according to the farm, during which period the ewes are brought down to the inland, though on some farms they run with the ewes on the fells, the gimmer shearlings being bratted – it used to be customary not to put the latter to the ram till they were 3½ years old. The tups are always coloured red at this season of the year to enable the ewes to find them on the open fells – red clay from Red Tarn was formerly used for the purpose, the getting of which was let with the farm, now red ochre is used. Lanty Slee, the last of the illicit distillers in the Lake District, who died in 1878, discovered a vein of 'rud' in the Langdale Fells, which he mined and sold for 'rudding' the sheep – on delivery it was often known to have some of 't'udder stuff' concealed in it.

JANE ROUTLEDGE GOODFELLOW LAUDER AT WOODSIDE

SHEEPSHEARING AT BAINSBANK, MIDDLETON, KIRKBY LONSDALE

The lambing season commences about the second week in April and continues till the latter part of May. Herdwicks are not great breeders, about 10 per cent of the ewes have twins, and if well done this percentage is increased; about 90 lambs to 100 ewes put to the tup is considered good and 80 not bad. Young poor ewes are sometimes shy about suckling their lambs, and when they are short of milk a little cow's milk is given to the lambs as a substitute – it is prevented from curding by scalding it with a piece of red hot tile or iron.

Some of the older ewes are drafted each season and put to Border Leicester rams, or what is now looked upon as even a better cross by many shrewd farmers, a Wensleydale – though the lambs do not fatten quite so early. Formerly the ewes were kept as long as they would breed, 15 or 16 years if they lived so long, but now they are drafted after four to six crops have been taken, and then sold to lower situated farms where they are put to Down, Leicester, Border Leicester, or Wensleydale tups, and the lambs sold fat the following autumn – lambs of the Leicester-Herdwick cross were sold fat during August and September, 1872, for 25s. to 30s. each, but that was a very favourable season. Some farmers keep such lambs till after they are clipped, the fleece weighing 7 to 8 lbs, which was worth 1/6 per lb in 1874 – afterwards selling them fat for 38s. to 45s. each.

Wethers were never sold before they were 4½ to 5½ years old, but now they go off as lambs and shearlings – but few being kept till they are twinters, such is the fashion for early maturity and the saving of keep, beside the lessened loss in the stock. The practice of sending the hogs to lower lands as near the sea as possible for the winter is still pursued; the price which, when Pringle wrote, was 2/- per head for those that returned in the spring, inceased to about 3/6 per head in 1850, and was from 7/- to 8/- in 1874; it is now 6/- to 7/- per head, with the same conditions pertaining. The 5th of April, on which they are returned, is known as 'Hog Day.'

Many of the noted Herdwick breeders keep a large number of rams, the price of which, in the eighties, ranged from £2 to £6, though noted animals brought much more. Favourite rams are sometimes hired for the season at from £7 to £10. At the Keswick Tup Fair, held on November 5th, 1870, E. Nelson, of Gatesgarth, had 40 tups on view, and sold or let all but three – his famous tup, 'Boggle,' was let for seven days at £1 per day, and for other ten days for £7. 136 Herdwick ewes, belonging to J. Pearson of Low Lorton, averaged £1 19s. 7d. each in 1873, and his tups made up to £12 10s.

At a sale of Herdwicks at the Boot, Troutbeck, in 1876, the following average prices were recorded: Ewes, 35/5; gimmer twinters, 33/11; gimmer hogs, 23/8; 3 and 4 year old wethers,

WYTHBURN AND HELVELLYN FROM THE CITY

31/10; wether twinters, 22/11; and wether hogs, 16/1. Higher prices were recorded in 1889 at a sale of Gillbank's heaf-going Herdwicks from Grasmere and Wythburn. At a sale of Herdwick sheep at Ambleside Fair in 1890, from Hartsop Hall, wethers averaged 25/6, wether twinters 22/-, wether lambs 12/6, gimmer twinters 28/-, and stock ewes 29/-.

Herdwicks were first shown at an exhibition of the Royal Agricultural Society, when the meeting was held at Carlisle in 1855; of the three prizes offered all came to Westmorland, through Geo. Robinson of Orton and John Mounsey of Askham, both on the very borders of the Herdwick country. In 1864 the Royal was at Newcastle, when there were 16 entries of Herdwicks, 13 of which were from Cumberland and three from Westmorland, and the chief winners were: Geo. Browne of Troutbeck and Ed. Nelson of Gatesgarth. In 1869 there were 19 entries at Manchester in three classes, when Geo. Browne and Richard Browne of Troutbeck and Ed. Nelson were again the chief winners. It was at this show that the celebrated ram, 'Nero,' then 3 years and 2 months' old, won in the aged class; he was afterwards sold for £30. At Liverpool, 1877, there were 18 entries in three classes, when E. Nelson, Geo. Browne and Wm. Leathes of Lamplugh Hall were the winners. There was a large entry when the Royal was again at Carlisle in 1880, where the chief winners were

Ed. Hawell of Lonscale, John Newby (Muncaster Head), Geo. Browne, and Ed. Nelson. Each year since 1893 there have been classes for Herdwicks at the Royal, though on several occasions the competition has been very poor. At the third visit of the Royal to Carlisle, in 1902, there were 23 entries in three classes, John Bennett of Cleator won in the two-shear and upwards class with 'Hero,' while Wm. Mackereth, Ambleside, won the premium for shearling rams with 'King Moor' and also for the best pen of three shearling ewes. At the four previous Royal Shows the number of entries were: 1898, 6; 1899, 2; 1900, 6; and 1901, 8.

F.W. Garnett

TO SHEPHERDS

If you wish to find out any particular Farmer, and cannot find him in the Township in which you expect to find his name, refer to the adjoining Township, as there are instances in which my information has been obtained from parties who were not quite sure of the divisional line of Townships; and sometimes the name of the Township in which the sheep run is inserted in place of that in which the Farmstead is situated.

ROSE COTTAGE, BAILEY, BEWCASTLE

Some few Stocks are entered by the Landlord, and are therefore entered in his name.

There are several Entries still unpaid; but trusting to the honour of the Parties concerned, I have inserted them in order to make the work as complete as possible.

Others there are who have entered their marks as differing one time from another; this, in my opinion is needless and inconvenient − were there many instances of this kind, *any* Guide would be imperfect and useless; whilst some others seem as if they could not have any definite marks, and are continually changing them; but I hope that, now this Guide is published, they will adhere strictly to the marks they have here entered.

A few districts have different terms for points and marks, but they are mostly entered as described by the Farmers themselves.

Some few have two distinct marks combined in one entry, therefore it is impossible to show them properly on the print of the Sheep.

All smits must be understood to be *red* unless otherwise stated.

The words 'ear mark various,' 'uncertain,' or 'no ear marks,' invariably apply to ewes that have been bought from different stocks, for breeding purposes.

In case any New Stock or Stocks are introduced in any Township, one or more spaces are left for their insertion.

On finding a stray sheep, I would recommend you to first look for corresponding earmarks in the print, then if the smits do not agree, search further; and if you do not find smits similar to those on the Sheep, communite with those farmers whose marks most nearly resemble them.

Any further Information may be obtained by applying to
DANIEL GATE, KESWICK.

Gates Shepherd's Guide for Cumberland, Westmorland and Lancashire

FARM SERVANTS

A return was made by John Crosby, of Kirkby Thore to the *Agricultural Gazette* in 1850 of wages paid for agricultural labour. The prices may be taken as those pertaining to the Bottom of Westmorland: Weekly wages of men, 11/-; ditto harvest time (with meat, drink and lodgings), 12/-; female labourers, daily wage 10d. to 1/-. Clover mowing, 2/- per acre. Meadow grass, 2/6 to 3/- per acre. Reaping wheat per acre, 7/- to 9/-. Thrashing and cleaning wheat per bushel, 3d. Digging per yard in length in clay sub-soil, $3\frac{1}{2}$ feet deep 14 inches wide at the top, and 3 inches at the bottom, 1d. to $1\frac{1}{4}$d. Ordinary cottage rent, 50/- to 60/- per year.

KIRKBY THORE

In Government publications issued in 1900, 1905, and 1910 the average adult male labourer's wage in Westmorland, including allowances of every description, such as board and lodging, which was taken as equivalent to 8/- per week, was 18/9, 20/-, and 19/9 per week in the years 1898, 1903, and 1907 respectively.

Casual labourers or 'darrickers' are employed only to a small extent and usually live in cottages in the adjacent villages to where they are employed, not infrequently they board with the farmer. From returns made by the Rural District Councils the rate of cash wages for such labourers per week was:

	1895		1897		1903	
	Jan.	June.	Jan.	June.	Jan.	June.
East Ward R.D.C.	16/-	16/-	16/6	18/-	19/-	19/6
South Westmorland R.D.C.	20/-	20/-	20/-	20/-	20/-	21/-
West Ward R.D.C.	15/-	15/-	15/-	15/6	17/-	18/-

These rates are exclusive of all extras and allowances. In the East and West Wards in many cases free cottages are provided, in some cases with gardens; potatoes and milk are allowed in other cases.

The scarcity of cottages accounts to a large extent for the custom of boarding and lodging the labourers in the farm-house – the custom enables both male and female servants to save a considerable proportion of their wage, which is carefully laid by each year with a view to marriage and taking a small farm on leaving service; but although Westmorland must be

accounted a county of small holdings, there is much competition for them, and the rents are so high for the quality of the land, that many of the best men are forced to emigrate each year.

In the Annual Report for 1868 of the Penrith Branch of the Carlisle Savings' Bank the amount due to 260 male farm servants was £9,259 9s. 5d., and to 240 female farm servants £7,904 8s. 9d. In the Kirkby Lonsdale, Morland, Shap, Appleby, Kirkby Stephen, and Temple Sowerby Lodges of Friendly Societies there were, in 1868, 364 farm servants and farm labourers members.

Women have been employed in outdoor farm labour to a greater extent than is desirable, especially during the first three quarters of the century, though it has been on a continually decreasing scale. In 1794 Pringle reported that it was 'painful to behold the beautiful servant maids of the district toiling in the severe labours of the field; they drive the harrow and the plough, when they are drawn by three horses; nay, it is not uncommon to see, toiling at the dung carts a girl whose elegant features and delicately-proportioned limbs but ill accord with such rough treatment.' Henry Tremenheere of Grasmere, one of the assistant commissioners to the Royal Commission on the Employment of Women and Children in Agriculture, reported, in 1869, that the greater part of such work as spreading dung, weeding crops, thinning turnips, and taking up potatoes is still done by female farm servants and by extra women when they can be procured. About 20 years previously the public agricultural gang system had been introduced, and there existed in Penrith eight public gang

OAKSHAW, CLATTERING FORD, BEWCASTLE

CROOKBURN FOOT, BAILEY, BEWCASTLE

WEST CUMBERLAND HARVEST

masters and seven women carrying on the same business, who employed about 300 young women and children of the lowest class. Tremenheere found that they were not properly looked after while they were at work, and that their education was neglected; they were sent out in gangs of 20 to 40 to the larger arable farms, the age of the children was from ten years upwards, and they received a penny a 100 yards for turnip thinning. The gangs were kept fairly employed for about eight months of the year. Private gangs also existed in the county wherever large arable farms prevailed. The Act of 1867, which required a licence for the gangmasters, had not been enforced at Penrith. Tremenheere met the magistrates and informed them of the provisions of the Act which they promised should be enforced in future.

'There are very few women workers now,' writes a Westmorland correspondent to the *Agricultural Gazette* in 1880, 'owing to high wages. A few women, for thinning turnips, get 2d. per hundred yards. The best hired women do not go out of the house, though many milk and serve the calves and go into the hay-fields.'

The diet of farm servants, about 1870, was the same as the rest of the household – all sitting down at the same table. Breakfast consisted of porridge made of milk; 'drinking' about 10 a.m. of bread and cheese with beer or milk, this was taken out to the men wherever they might happen to be working;

dinner at noon of fruit pudding or if plain with treacle sauce, followed by meat, baked, boiled or made into pies with potatoes and other vegetables; 4 p.m. tea, taken out to the men, of bread and cheese or tea and bread and butter with jam or pasties; supper of bread and cheese or porridge, without stint. The bread was composed of two-thirds best wheaten flour and one-third rye. Beer was but rarely given, and tea was little used.

The labour of a farm hand in Westmorland is hard, and the hours are long, but the food is good and sufficient, and both men and women are well fitted for their work – they are healthy and strong, the pity is so many are forced to emigrate through lack of small holdings.

After considerable agitation through their clubs and discussion by the County Council, for the compulsory production of 'character books,' which had no effect, the farmers started a system on a voluntary basis at the Whitsuntide hirings at Kendal in 1909, the local farmers' club having issued books for the purpose to all its members. The experiment was not a success. It is related that a lad having agreed to hire with a farmer, the latter said he would meet him again after he had got his character. On this taking place, the farmer said, 'I'se gitten thee character an its aw reet me lad.' 'I, an I'se gitten thine, an I'se nut gaan,' was the reply.

F.W. Garnett

THRESHING AT SELSIDE HALL, NEAR KENDAL

MARKETS AND FAIRS

1899 – Kendal Market January 7th   May 7th   Sept. 2nd

Oats, per stone of 14lbs	10½d.	11d.	1/-
Flour, " "	1/6	1/5	1/5
Oatmeal " "	1/9	1/9	1/9
Butter, per lb	1/4½d.	1/-	1/3½d.
Potatoes, per stone	5½d.	6d.	5½d.
Beef, per lb	4d. to 9d.	4d. to 9d.	4d. to 9d.
Mutton "	6d. to 9d.	6½d. to 9½d.	6d. to 8d.
Lamb, "	–	1/- to 1/2	7½d. to 9d.
Hams, "	9½d.	8½d.	9½d.
Pork (live), per stone	4/-	4/-	4/3
Young Pigs, each	20/-	28/-	22/-
Hay, per stone	7d.	7d.	7d.
Oat straw, per stone	4½d.	4½d.	4½d.
Ducks, each	2/6 to 3/6	2/6 to 3/6	2/6 to 3/6
Hens, "	1/- to 2/-	1/- to 1/9	1/- to 1/9
Chickens, "	1/9 to 2/9	2/3 to 3/3	1/9 to 2/9
Rabbits, "	8d. to 1/2	8d. to 1/-	8d. to 1/-
Eggs, hens	8 to 9 for 1/-	16 to 17 for 1/-	9 to 10 for 1/-
Eggs, ducks	6 to 7 for 1/-	13 to 14 for 1/-	8 for 1/-

TRACTION ENGINE, NEAR BROUGHTON-IN-FURNESS

F.W. Garnett

63

TILBERTHWAITE, CONISTON

JOHN RUSKIN

The road to Brantwood runs beneath the old trees which shade the head of Coniston Water, and you leave the village and the inn behind, and the Thwaite, with its pretty old gardens and peacocks, and skirt the beautiful grounds of Monk Coniston; you pass the ivy tower where the lords of the manor keep their boats, and the reeds among which the swallows and dragon-flies are darting; and as you advance, if you look back across the green hayfields and wooded slopes of Monk Coniston, you can see Wetherlam and Ravenscrag, with Yewdale for a background, while Coniston Old Man on the opposite side of the lake rises like a Pilatus above the village, and soars into changing lights and clouds. Then, as you walk still farther along the road, leaving all these things behind, you pass into a sweet Arcadia, in which, indeed, one loses one's self again in after-times. You go by Tent Lodge, where Tennyson once dwelt, where the beautiful Romneys are hanging on the walls; you pass the cottage with roses for bricks, and with jasmines and honey-suckles for thatch, and the farm where the pet lamb used to dwell, to the terror of the children (it seemed appropriate enough to Wordsworth country, but I can remember a little baby girl wild with terror and flying from its

gambols); then, still following the road, you reach a delightful cackling colony of poultry and ducks, where certain hospitable ladies used to experimentalise, and prove to us whether or no eggs are eggs (as these ladies have determined eggs should be); then comes Low Bank Ground, our own little farm, wedging among the chestnut-trees and meadows full of flowers. It had been the site of a priory once, and on this slope and in the shade of the chestnut-trees, where monks once dwelt, the writer met Ruskin again after many years. He, the master of Brantwood, came, as I remember, dressed with some ceremony, meeting us with a certain old-fashioned courtesy and manner; but he spoke with his heart, of which the fashion doesn't change happily from one decade to another; and as he stood in his tall hat and frock-coat upon the green, the clouds and drifts came blowing up from every quarter of heaven, and I can almost see him still, and hear the tones of his voice as he struck the turf with his foot, speaking with emphasis and true and hospitable kindness. Low Bank Ground is but a very little way from Brantwood; you can go there by land or by water. If you walk, the road climbs the spur of the hill, and runs below moors along a wood where squirrels sit under the oak-trees and honey-suckles drop from the branches; or, if you like to go by the lake, you can get Timothy from the farm to row

FELLGATE COTTAGE AND GARDEN, WOODLAND

you. 'A dash of the oars and you are there,' as Ruskin said, and accordingly we started in the old punt for our return visit to Brantwood.

The sun came out between rain-clouds as the boat struck with a hollow crunch against the stones of the tiny landing-pier. Timothy from the farm, who had come to pilot us, told us, with a sympathetic grin, that Mr Ruskin – 'Rooskin,' I think he called him – 'had built t' pier, and set t' stoans himsel' wi' the other gentlemen, but they had to send for t' smith from the village to make the bolts fawster.' The pier is fast enough, running out into the lake, with a little fleet safely anchored behind it, while Brantwood stands high up on the slope, with square windows looking across the waters. Just on the other side of the lake, wrapped in mysterious ivy wreaths, where the cows are whisking their tails beneath the elms, rise the gables of the old farm, once the manor-house where 'Sidney's sister, Pembroke's mother,' once dwelt. Sir Philip Sidney used to come riding across the distant hills to visit her there – so tradition says. The mere thought of Coniston Water brings back the peaceful legends and sounds all about Ruskin's home – the wash of the lake, the rustle of the leaves and

rushes, the beat of birds on their whirring wings, the flop of the water-rats, the many buzzing and splashing and delicious things. A path up a garden of fruit and flowers, of carnations and strawberries, leads with gay zigzags to the lawn in front of the Brantwood windows.

The house is white, plain, and comfortable, absolutely unpretending. I remember noticing with a thrill the umbrella-stand in the glass door. So Mr Ruskin had an umbrella just like other people! It seemed to me to be a dwelling planned for sunshine, and sunshine on the lakes is of a quality so sweet and rare that it counts for more than in any other place. The brightness of Brantwood, the squareness, and its unaffected comfortableness, were, I think, the chief characteristics. You had a general impression of solid, old-fashioned furniture, of amber-coloured damask curtains and coverings; there were Turners and other water-colour pictures in curly frames upon the drawing-room walls – a Prout, I think, among them; there was a noble Titian in the dining-room, and the full-length portrait of a child in a blue sash over the sideboard has become familiar since then to the readers of *Praeterita*; and most certainly was there an absence of any of the art-diphthongs

65

DUDDON HALL GARDENS

and peculiarities of modern taste: only the simplest and most natural arrangments for the comfort of the inmates and their guests, − Turkey carpets, steady round tables, and above all a sense of cheerful, hospitable kindness, which seems to be traditional at Brantwood. For many years past Mrs Severn has kept her cousin's house, and welcomed his guests with her own.

That evening, the first we ever spent at Brantwood, the rooms were lighted by slow sunset cross-lights from the lake without. Mrs Severn sat in her place behind a silver urn, while the master of the house, with his back to the window, was dispensing such cheer, spiritual and temporal, as those who have been his guests will best realise, − fine wheaten bread and Scotch cakes in many a crisp circlet and crescent, and trout from the lake, and strawberries such as grow only on the Brantwood slopes. Were these cups of tea only, or cups of fancy, feeling, inspiration? And as we crunched and quaffed we listened to a certain strain not easily to be described, changing from its graver first notes to the sweetest and most charming vibrations.

Anne Ritchie

LOCAL ANECDOTES, BY FURNESSIAN

No Admittance

Two Ulverstonians (one of whose name commenced with K) were indulging in a very heated argument which became more personal every moment, when one them wound up by saying, 'Well, at any rate, I've the satisfaction of knowing there's no possibility of *you* ever going to heaven?' 'For why!' asked the other. 'Well,' continued the first speaker, 'We are told most distinctly in the Bible, there shall be no *night* there?'

May Gosling

An old O'ostan worthy, exceedingly fond of using long words but not so well able to pronounce them, was perusing the dictionary in search of knowledge, when he chanced to light on the word 'magazine,' he forthwith proceeded to spell the word very slowly, and ended in pronouncing it 'May Gesslin.' His eye then fell upon the meaning of the word as given in the dictionary − a place used for storing gunpowder. 'By gox,' he exclaimed in astonishment, 'I nivver knew that afoore.'

OXENHOPE PACK OF OTTER HOUNDS, DALLAM, MILNTHORPE

Rather Facetious

A local artist employed in repainting the signboard of the Inn at Oxen Park, known as the 'Black Lion,' had just finished his work, having made anything but a faithful likeness of the King of Beasts, as the following will testify, when he was accosted by an old resident, as follows: 'Well, thou's finished thy job' – after a pause during which he eyed the sign critically – 'thou'll likely be putting a verse under it next?' 'Nay!' said the artist, 'I don't think I can make owt up to suit.' 'Why, at any rate,' said the first speaker, 'thou can console thysel' wi' this, that thou hessent brocken any o't commandments o'er painting on it?' 'How's that!' queried the artist. 'Why,' returned his critical friend, 'Thou hessent made for thysel' t' likeness of owt in Heaven above, or in't earth beneath, or in't watters under t' earth, so thou's o' reet.'

Caught

A man with only one eye, hailing not far from Greenodd, offered to bet a friend of his that he (the one-eyed person) could see more than the other. The bet was accepted. 'You have lost,' said the first, 'for I can see *two* eyes in your head, whilst you can only see *one* in mine?'

Going Down

A certain old gentleman on his death-bed observed to his old coachman, who was in attendance on him, 'Ah, John, I am going a longer journey now than ever you drove me?' 'Why,' replied John, 'nivver heed that, its o' down hill.'

Mackereth's Year Book, 1897

THE CARRIER

One scene characteristic of Lakeland comes before us at the outskirts of the little town. It is the country carrier, a lusty, embrowned, genial man, and his large covered cart within which in picturesque (but safe) confusion are the parcels from a larger town to our vale. Storm or calm, rain, shine, or snow, so regular that events are timed by his appearances, passes the carrier along the roads of this land where are no railways. An old farmer, selling some sheep to a dealer, asked when he would take away his purchase.

'Will it do if I come about the seventh of next month?'

'Oh aye,' but the old man looked puzzled. After the dealer had taken his leave, a reflective voice sounded from the ingle-nook.

'T' seventh o' next month! That'll be—' and for awhile the old farmer counted on his fingers, but without satisfaction to himself.

'That'll be t' Tuesday after t' carrier comes, father,' announced a matron who was washing dishes at the far end of the room.

'Aye,' responded the old man promptly, 'that'll be three weeks to-morn; t' sheep'll be ready.'

This is not an extraordinary thing to hear in our dales where the list of 'inevitables' is: Rent-day, Candlemas (February 2nd, when all accounts are rendered), *and* t' Carrier.

The carrier's life is an arduous one, yet we have whole families who succeed one another in it without a break. Our oldest 'carrier' family is to be traced in manor-rolls far into the pack-horse days. The halting of the railway on the confines of

NETHERBY STREET, LONGTOWN

Lakeland has preserved, and indeed given impetus to, his craft. He is a necessity to dales-life, but now he is perhaps doomed to totally disappear. The new traffic companies are hoping to send their motors, humming and throbbing, with loads of parcels into the villages and over the passes. As a rule our carrier is a genial soul – he knows the gossip of a hundred miles of road. 'We can neither stir dish nor spoon,' complain the daleswomen (who are keenest to hear his news and give notes of their neighbours), 'wi'out the carrier hearin' on it.'

Wm T. Palmer

A RESTORED INDUSTRY

In most of the recent exhibitions that have been devoted to handicrafts – notably in that just lately held by the Society of Arts and Crafts, there has been at least one case containing specimens of needlework executed on unbleached or partially bleached linen in all its delicate shades of cream colour. This material, known as Langdale linen, takes its name from the Westmoreland Valley where it is made. It is entirely spun and woven by hand, and is bleached in the open air without the aid of chemicals.

It was ten years last Easter since the first piece of it – looking marvellously like sacking – was taken off the loom; the seed then sewn had yielded due increase, and now about one hundred persons are altogether employed in spinning, weaving and embroidering, besides a few who attend to correspondence and business arrangements.

From the first moment when my friend, Albert Fleming, intimated that he intended to restore this lost industry to the cottages near his home in the beautiful Langdale Valley, I have been a deeply interested spectator. At first, like most other people, though admiring the attempt, I was incredulous as to its stability or ultimate success; and before the linen reached the stage of being taken off the loom it had gone through an amount of difficulties and vicissitudes that seemed to justify the sceptics.

For some years before the revival of the Langdale hand-spinning, Mr Fleming had been in possession of a little ebony spinning-wheel, and was in the habit of challenging his lady friends to prove by its use their possession of those feminine domestic graces that have adorned the immemorial woman from Solomon and Homer onwards, until her prerogatives have been lost among modern machinery. It was not so much the test of womanly virtue as he individually conceived it: the little black wheel was rather used as a sort of Ruskin banner,

LITTLE LANGDALE SCHOOL

the advance guard and ensign of all that Mr Ruskin has said concerning the superiority of hand labour, and the qualifications that he deems essential in the character of a noble woman. He has scattered passages bearing more or less directly on these subjects through the literary work of almost half a century; but it is in the *Fors Clavigera* he has so far formulated his theories as to give his disciples a basis on which they can build up work which may help forward the ends that he has in view. In one of the letters that compose the book, he says, that looking over his notes on the projected Sheffield Museum he finds one to the effect that he would exhibit there 'All that is reasonable, illustrating the true nature of a thread and a needle – then the phase of its spinning, then the mystery of weaving, and finally the accomplished phase of needlework.' He adds – 'Very thankfully I can now say that this vision of thread and needlework, though written when my fancy had too much possession of me, is now being, in all its branches, realised by two greatly valued friends; the spinning on the old spinning-wheel with most happy and increasingly acknowledged results systematised here among our Westmoreland Hills by Mr Albert Fleming; the useful sewing by Miss Stanley of Whitelands College. I am not sure that Mr Fleming ever met with a single friend who could so much as tell him whether his spinning-wheel was complete. I am sure that when a wheel in working order had been obtained from the Isle of Man – where they are to a limited extent still in use – and a bundle of flax had been received from Ireland, there was no member of his circle of friends who had any clear idea as to how a connection could be established between the one and the other.

ABIGAIL PEPPER SPINNING

ELIZABETH PEPPER AT THE LOOM

A few inquiries in the village discovered an old woman of more than ninety years who had not forgotten the employments of her youth, and she taught Mr Fleming and one or two enterprising ladies to spin. I was myself merely a spectator, being engaged in other work, and for one who was willing to look on, there were at least six eager to set their hands to the spindle and the distaff, and at that time only one wheel available.

It soon became clear that to learn how to spin was one thing, and to accomplish the making of a good thread another. To a spectator the thing is simplicity itself; a wheel with two bands passing round the spindle, one of them turns the bobbin, the other twists the thread. You have only to work the wheel with your foot while you draw out a regular quantity of flax, either from the distaff, or from a mass held in the left hand, and pass it unbroken and free from tangle between the fingers and thumb of your right hand towards the bobbin. Practically it takes most people about a fortnight to learn to make a good, even reliable thread. At first the treadle is not easy to work, the wheel reverses, then goes in jerks, your foot cannot keep pace with your hands, your hands give out the flax in lumps and fragile fibres. Then the bands get loose, the spindle does not draw, the thread does not twist, it comes all to pieces, the bands slip off altogether; tighten them well up and the wheel will not go round. It needed a good deal of patience from both teacher and pupils, and the revival was undertaken only just in time to save the industry from total oblivion in the Langdale Valley. Our old lady seemed to recall some of the details with an effort, and there was but one

other, some six or seven miles away, who had any recollection of it. When these two met there was a very animated discussion between them as to whether it was best to spin from the distaff or the hand, each being convinced that the other was wrong.

As soon as the spinning was set on foot there was a great searching for wheels all through the country-side. Two or three delightfully picturesque old ones were presented by Lady Bective; a few more were heard of in outlying country cottages. These last were the objects of very pleasant drives, but in most cases when they were discovered they turned out to be so broken, imperfect or worm-eaten that this part of the quest was abandoned, and the village carpenter, who had some mechanical skill, was commissioned to imitate the one that had been made in the Isle of Man.

Wheels, flax and some experience having been secured, the first step may fairly be said to have been taken, but the next was more difficult, and I must own that we who looked on sometimes thought that the attempt to bring into practical form the ideal theories of Mr Ruskin would go no farther, not perhaps quite realising that a sum of two hundred pounds had been dedicated to the venture and that to that extent, at the very least, the attempt was made in sober earnest. In the first place we all said that there was no demand for hand-made linen. People appeared to be perfectly content with what they could buy in the ordinary way, and even supposing that a really superior article could be produced in the old method, which result seemed exceedingly remote, it must be at an enormously advanced price, and we thought that the country-

people would look upon it as a mere fad, and would hardly be inclined to give up time enough to it to get over the initial difficulties.

At this point a lady who had known Mr Fleming for many years, and who was then living in the Langdale Valley, offered to help in organising the industry, and for about six years she filled the position of practical manager.

From Mr Fleming's house, which is situated on the top of a high rock on the fell-side, you can look up the course of the Brathay as it flows through the green meadows, and beyond the Brathay across the little triple lake of Elterwater to the village of the same name. Here a suitable cottage was found and newly-christened St Martin's, after the saint who divided his cloak with a beggar. It is a 17th-century little place with a wood clothing the rising ground behind it and a rocky stream within fifty yards of it. In this home the industry was started on a business footing. The country women were taught to spin, and as soon as they were at all competent, wheels were lent to them, flax was given out and the yarn paid for by weight. They soon saw the advantage of a home employment by which they could earn five or six shillings a week, and which could be taken up in leisure moments without interfering with domestic duties. When a loom and a weaver had been with some difficulty found and established in an outbuilding, it may fairly be said that the scheme had struck root. Even then there was much discouragement to be faced; enthusiasm was the oil that made the wheels go round, for there was a very laborious as

well as a picturesque side to the undertaking. All the workers had everything to learn. At first only two or three could spin a strong useful yarn, several others were with great trouble and patience slowly producing a lumpy unequal thread, rotten in parts and in others resembling a very bad piece of string. The wheels, like all the tools of the inexperienced workmen, took strange freaks, the bands continually slipped off, or a message would come down to St Martin's that such and such wheels would not work. These little aberrations often meant evening walks to outlying cottages to give practical help and encouragement, and the purchase of a good deal of thread that never found its way into any web.

The first bobbins that reached the weaver were a marvel of variety. There were threads of such diverse qualities that they could by no means be used on the same piece of cloth, thread that was so unequal and rotten that by the time the weaver had examined, cut and joined and made it ready for use he had spent almost as much time on it as if he had spun it himself, thread bad beyond all possibility of utilisation. After many failures and discouragements it was a proud and triumphant moment when the first web of about sixteen yards was taken off the loom, an event so important that it was especially reserved for Easter Sunday, albeit to the uninitiated it appeared only like a piece of dark-coloured sacking exceedingly uneven at the edges.

In those early days the cult of the spinning-wheel had a picturesque romance and enthusiasm about it that has now

ON THE FELL NEAR BURTON-IN-KENDAL

settled down into a businesslike utilitarianism. Votaries rose early in the morning, and while the web of the perennial spider hung dew-laden on the heather the shining flax sped between the rosy finger-tips of the temporary Arachne and added its quota to the roll of accomplished handiwork. The whirr of the wheel pervaded the morning dream, and accompanied readings from the poets in the evening. Those who did not spin became quite the exceptions. Even the young Hercules, whose latest feat had been the ascent of five mountains in one long summer day, sat down to the spinning-wheel to try his skill. Other enthusiasts finished breakfast with extraordinary celerity, fetched a wheel, poured water into one of the saucers, moistened their fingers, and had done yards of thread while the lookers-on were discussing their second eggs and the plans for the day. In the evening, when we were on the lake, and noting the glow in the sky and the deepening purple of the mountains, a boat would draw up alongside, and we would hear a gentle undercurrent of talk concerning bobbins, wheels, looms, and treadles, qualities of thread, and rates of payment.

At any time of the day groups of people might be seen gazing in rapt admiration at what appeared to be a big piece of calico laid upon the ground, or crowded into the bathroom, washing the precious fabric with their own hands. Once too every available piece of it was carried to a specially picturesque, but in truth remarkably rocky, field, that there, amongst the very choicest surroundings, in full view of the stretch of the Langdale Valley and the misty blue mass of its Pikes, the linen might be bleached by the sun, and the wind,

BROUGHTON MILLS

72

NEAR DUDDON HALL

and the purifying dew. Surely, if inanimate things can indeed imbibe anything of the human interest that has gone out to them during their creation, those first hand-spun and woven sheets should bring wonderful dreams to their possessors, although a Philistine critic said, when he saw them, that he could match the material with his cook's apron.

The spinning industry once established the work progressed steadily, and it did not seem long before Mr Fleming was able to send out from St Martin's specimens of different qualities of linen to his customers. At first he overlooked the work himself, visiting the little home daily while in Westmoreland, wrote articles for magazines, and endless letters, and made it known in every way. It soon became evident that there was an actual demand for the hand-made linen, notwithstanding its high price, even in its very crudest form. The first piece was immediately purchased, and the orders have always exceeded the production.

Mr Fleming's original idea was to make sheets which should restore long-lost qualities of solid endurance, and these are still made, but as time went on and the linen became a really beautiful fabric it found a place of its own. A lady who has a great talent for needlework, recognised its special capabilities, both of colour and texture as a foundation and background for silk or flax thread embroidery, and for the open stitches called Greek lace. She has now quite a large number of ladies engaged in working on it. They embroider quilts, curtains, tea-cloths, *portières* and all sorts of smaller articles. Most of the work is at the headquarters of the industry, St Martin's, Elterwater, near Ambleside; some of it has not returned from the Chicago Exhibition, where it has received an award. A material which is a mixture of white silk and unbleached linen was worked in white silk, a cream coloured linen was embroidered with silk of precisely the same tone. Many other pieces of work are executed in brilliant and beautiful colours. The industry is still spreading; there are several off-shoots in England, and three or four in Ireland.

The Girl's Own Paper

'FOND OF HIS "LICKER"' AT BARROW

INCIDENT IN A LOCAL POLICE COURT

Solicitor, examining unwilling witness: He was drunk, was he not?

Witness: No, he wasn't drunk.

Solicitor: Was he sober?

Witness: He might, for owt I knah.

Solicitor: Was he sober, or was he not?

Witness: Its hard to say. Mebbe he was, mebbe he wasn't.

Solicitor: Now, this fencing won't do. Was this man under the influence of liquor?

Witness: Ah cannot say, ahm sure.

Solicitor: You saw him on the occasion in question?

Witness: Yes, ah sah him, leastwise if it wasn't him it was somebody varra like him.

Solicitor: Very well, I'll put the question again, and be careful what you say. Was he under the influence of drink?

Witness: Ah nivvor sah him hev ony drink.

Solicitor: You are not asked if you saw him have drink. You are asked if he was under the influence of liquor.

Witness: Hoo kan ah tell, when ah nivvor sah him hev ony drink. (Laughter).

Solicitor (savagely): Did he stagger?

Witness: What hes that got ta dew wi' it?

Solicitor: You must answer, not ask questions, my man. Say now, was he staggering?

Witness: Ah dar say he wod.

Solicitor (fiercely): Was he staggering?

Witness: Yis, hevn't ah said soa afoore?

Solicitor: Then how did you come to say he was not drunk?

Witness (emphatically): He wasn't drunk, whativver else he mod be.

Solicitor: Not drunk and staggering?

Witness: A man can stagger wi'out being drunk, sewer-lie.

Magistrate: There are differences of opinion about drunkenness. Say, was he the worse for drink?

Witness: Ah was ex'd that afore by t' 'torney, an ah telt him ah didn't knah. If ah knahed, ah wud tell ye willingly, yer honour.

Solicitor: Then you consider that when a man takes sufficient drink to make him stagger he is no worse for it?

Witness: No, ah didn't say that. What ah said was that ah didn't knah if he hed heny drink in him, how kan ah say he was the warse for't?

Magistrate: But if he staggered, would you not infer that he had had drink?

Witness: No; he might be bad, or lots o' things.

Solicitor: Did his breath smell?

Witness: Yes.

Solicitor: What did it smell like?

Witness: It smelled ahful bad.

Solicitor: Exactly, Did it smell of drink?

Witness: No, that ah cuddent say.

Solicitor: By the bye, did you think he was drunk at the time?

Witness (hesitatingly): Well, yes, mebby ah did.

Solicitor: Have you since had any reason for changing your opinion.

Witness: Yes.

Solicitor: What reason?

EGREMONT

Witness: Gud reeazun.
Solicitor: State your reason, man.
Witness: His ahn waurd.
Solicitor: And that is your only reason?
Witness: That's ho ah can think on. It's gud enough, isn't it? He owt to knah best.
Solicitor: Very well, you may go.

Roger Piketah

AN AMUSING GRINNING MATCH

This wicked world is made up of many peculiar people, who are possessed of some very curious and peculiar forms of entertainment. Amongst the many funny things placed before a crowd of onlookers, for approbation and edification, none seems to strike me as being more objectionable, than individuals in competitions, pulling their faces into the most abhorrent shapes, for the express purpose of amusing a batch of idle spectators. There was always however at the races, a contest for those who like to enter, for one pound of tobacco (miserable prize for a miserable purpose), for the one who could screw his handsome physiogomy into the most vile shape. One consolation creeps into my conscience about this contest, memory or information avails me not in trying to bring forward a local person, whoever became possessor of this prize. As regular as the contest came round, a great raw-boned Irishman succeded in gaining the one pound of tobacco. His success was history in the locality, and finally no competitor was

forthcoming to tackle this valiant fascial contortionist in the open ring, which eventually resulted in him being barred out of the match. He however sturdy and true, like an old warrior, could not forbear visiting the field as a spectator, where he had once performed successfully as a competitor for the prize, and who became an anxious and ardent spectator of the competitors, who where struggling for the laurels he had so often won. He must as an onlooker have grinned unconsciously with some effect. The judge, a man of great integrity, after careful consideration of the performances of the india-rubber faced competitors, with a firm step and a stern face, one pound of tobacco in one hand, and his walking stick in the other, walked direct up to the Irishman, who was busy laughing and chaffing with his friends at the ring side, and presented the tobacco to him, at the same time telling him, that he had won it again, well and honestly, and hoped he would enjoy it. 'No! no!' exclaimed the Irishman, with some surprise 'I did not try for it.' 'Try or not try' returned the judge, 'it makes no difference, the prize is yours, here take it my man, when you are anywhere round about, nobody else has a chance.' The judge then thrust the tobacco into the Irishman's hands, who was not under the circumstances in a humour to take it, as he did not agree with the judge's decision, eventually, as the judge had walked off out of sight, he became reconciled to it, filled up his pipe, had a smoke, and as he watched the clouds of smoke curling in the air, probably turned over in his mind, the wisdom of the judge, who declared him the winner of a prize, for which he was not a competitor.

Joseph Fisher

'THE WIFE IS THE KEY OF THE HOUSE'

Husbands and Wives

Hints to Husbands – *Don't think when you have won a wife* that you have got, also, a slave.

Don't think that your wife has less feeling than your sweetheart. Her relationship to you is simply changed – not her nature.

Don't think you can dispense with all the little civilities of life towards her. She appreciates these things quite as much as other women.

Don't be gruff and rude at home. Had you been that sort of fellow before marriage, the probabilities are that you would be sewing on your own buttons still. Don't make your wife feel herself a burden on you by giving her grudgingly. What she needs give as cheerfully as if it were a pleasure for you to do so. She will feel much better, and so will you.

Don't meddle with the affairs of the house under her charge. You have no more right to be poking your nose into the kitchen than she to interfere with your employees.

Women soon tire of the company of men who are much at home. Men are wise in getting away from their own roof-trees a certain portion of each day. There will be found almost everywhere amongst wives a disposition to pack off the men in the morning, and to bid them keep out of the way till toward evening, when it is assumed that they will probably have a little news of the busy world to bring home, and when baby will be sure to have said something exceptionally brilliant and precocious.

ENSIGN AND MRS CLIFFORD, BARROW

WEDDING AT FIELD BROUGHTON, CARTMEL

Hints to Wives – *The following sensible hints to wives* are from the 'Memoirs of Isabel, Lady Burton':

Let your husband find in you a companion, friend and adviser, and confidante, that he may miss nothing at home.

Be a careful nurse when he is ailing, that he may never be in low spirits about his health without a serious cause.

Make his home snug. If it be ever so small and poor, there can always be a certain chic about it. Men are always ashamed of a poverty-striken home, and therefore prefer the club. Attend much to his creature comforts; allow smoking or anything else; for if you do not somebody else will. Make it yourself cheerful and attractive, and draw relations and intimates about him, and the style of society that suits him.

Improve and educate yourself in every way, that you may enter into his pursuits and keep pace with the times.

Do not try to hide your affection for him, but let him see and feel it in every action. Observe a certain amount of reserve and delicacy before him. Keep up the honeymoon romance, whether at home or in the desert. At the same time do not make prudish bothers, which only disgust and are not true modesty. Do not make the mistake of neglecting your personal appearance, but try to look well and dress well to please his eye.

Perpetually work up his interest with the world. Let him feel, when he has to go away, that he leaves a second self behind in charge of his affairs at home; so that if sometimes he is obliged to leave you behind, he may have nothing of anxiety on his mind. Take an interest in everything that interests him. To be

EVA PHILLIPS, 1908 ROSE QUEEN, ULVERSTON

WEDDING AT DERWENT HILL, PORTINSCALE, KESWICK

MR AND MRS COWARD, FOXFIELD

THE FAIRER FAMILY IN THE GARDEN AT HILLFIELD SHAP

companionable a woman must learn what interests her husband, and if it is only planting turnips, she must try to understand turnips.

Never confide your domestic affairs to your female friends.

Hide his faults from everyone, and back him up through every difficulty and trouble.

Never permit anyone to speak disrespectfully of him before you, and if any one does, no matter how difficult, leave the room. Never permit anyone to tell you anything about him, especially of his conduct with regard to other women.

Never open his letters, nor appear inquisitive about anything he does not volunteer to tell you.

Never interfere between him and his family; encourage their being with him, and forward everything he wishes to do for them, and treat them in every respect (as far as they will let you) as if they were your own.

A decent woman, says an English divine, came one market-day and begged to speak to me.

She told me, with an air of secrecy, that her husband behaved unkindly to her, and that knowing me to be a wise man I could tell her what would cure him.

'The remedy is simple,' I said. 'Always treat your husband with a smile.'

The women thanked me, dropped a curtsey, and went away.

A few months after she came again, bringing a couple of fine fowls. She told me with great satisfaction that I had cured her husband, and she begged my acceptance of the fowls in return. This was at once the victory of love and the reward of perseverance.

Mackereth's Year Book, 1897

THE WOODSIDE CHILDREN, WIGTON

ETIQUETTE FOR YOUNG PEOPLE

Politeness at Home – *To have young people courteous abroad* it is necessary that they should make the acquaintance of courteous manners at home. For the rudeness of their children fathers and mothers should often lay the blame on their own shoulders.

The child who lives in a refined home and is surrounded by elevating associations is necessarily more polite and polished in his manners than one who lives in a home where everything is done roughly, and where each one looks after and scrambles for himself. Pecuniary circumstances have nothing to do with the atmosphere of the home: the children of *rich* parents are frequently rude and uncouth; the children of *refined* parents are rarely so.

It must be understood, however, that the parent would be most unwise who trusted to the influence of association alone to form the manners of his children. There are certain little details of behaviour which need to be pointed out, and little observances to which attention must be called and which must be daily practised, before any child can become inured to the manners and customs of good society. Attention should be paid to these while children are yet quite young.

The easiest way for a child to learn to behave nicely at table is for him to take his meals regularly with those who are particular about behaviour, who notice at once any failure in good manners, and insist upon its correction. It is unreasonable to allow a child to behave carelessly every day and then be disappointed if on some particular occasion he displays his ill

SAILOR BOY, BARROW-IN-FURNESS

THREE GIRLS AT FELLGATE, WOODLAND

manners. If he is to be depended on to behave well in company, he must behave well regularly in private.

Whatever the customs of the family may be, it is a good thing for children to dine occasionally with their parents. Their manners can then be noticed, and if they are not quite what they ought to be, means should be taken to make them so.

Mackereth's Year Book, 1897

GOOD RULES FOR YOUNG FOLKS

Shut every door after you, and without slamming it. Never shout, jump, or run in the house. Never call to persons upstairs, or in the next rooms; if you wish to speak to them, go quietly where they are. Always speak kindly and politely to the servants if you would have them do the same to you. When told to do or not to do a thing, by either parent, never ask why you should or should not do it. Tell of your own faults and misdoings, not of those of your brothers and sisters. Carefully clean the mud or snow from your boots before entering the house. Be prompt at every meal hour. Never sit down at the table or in the parlour with soiled hands or tumbled hair. Never interrupt any conversation, but wait patiently your turn to speak. Never reserve your good manners for company, but be equally polite at home and abroad. Let your first, last, and best confidante be your mother.

Mackereth's Year Book, 1897

CHILDREN'S GAMES AS PLAYED AT KIRKOSWALD, CUMBERLAND

Read at Carlisle, June 20th, 1900

The following notes on traditional games and rhymes are offered as a contribution to what is now recognized as an interesting branch of folklore. My information has been obtained at first hand from the schoolchildren, and is here presented without comment as material for comparative study.

There is a regular sequence for the playing of most of the games at Kirkoswald, a sequence which seems to be determined mainly by the conditions of the weather and of the ground – hot, cold, wet, or dry. The following is a fairly complete list of all the outdoor games.

In spring, when snow is gone and the ground is dry, the girls begin to play with skipping-ropes, rounders, tiggie, girds and guiders, or girds and hooks (*i.e.*, hoops, the gird or girth being often a mere hoop from a cask); chucky-stones or clinks (knuckle-bones or dibs, though here we have no special names for the figures); and batty-ball, which consists in beating an elastic ball to the ground with the hand, to the accompaniment of a string of rhymes.

Later, they have their ring-games and dances, of which examples are given below.

The boys begin the season with marbles, a game for Lent, said to be originally intended to keep them from 'more boisterous and mischievous employment.' They play at buttons, rounders, whip (whoo-ip, hide and seek), top-spinning, kick-stone, guinea-pig (tipcat), nuts and crackers, lanty-loup and foot-and-a-half (two kinds of leap-frog).

In summer they add hattie (or egg-cap), blind-man's buff, puss-in-the-corner, pots and stones, flinches, duckie (duck-

NUNNERY WALKS, KIRKOSWALD

MARBLES AT ARNSIDE

stone), shows, horse-fairs, Adam and ish, hounds and hare, girds and guiders, tiggie-touchwood, finger and thumb, hitchy-pot (hop-scotch), and presently are added conkers or cobblers (played with chestnuts), batty-ball, rounders and marbles again, Roman soldiers, tally-ho.

In the hot weather the girls play whip, ball, three plain keps (elsewhere pots), trades, houses, schools, chitty (puss-in-corner), kick-stone. All the ring-games are still in season, with skipping-ropes, shuttle-cock, tally-ho, nuts and crackers, Roman soldiers, hounds and hare, half-past-catching-time. Prison-bars (prisoner's base) is played here as elsewhere. At Irthington they cry 'Chevy chase!'

In the cold weather the boys play their most athletic games to keep them warm: Horses, rounders, jumping, bull-break-out, chainey. Both sexes play 'Draw buckets of water,' and tiggie in all its varieties. In long-tiggie, called also horse-fairs, one pursues another and tigs or touches him, who must then join hands with the tigger. They pursue others until all are tigged or tug, and a long line is formed. In cross-tiggie, tiggee has to join hands cross-wise with tigger. In blind-tiggie, tigger shuts both eyes, so that this form becomes a kind of blind-man's buff. In lame-tiggie, tigger keeps the left hand raised and fixed close to the body. French-tiggie is a round game. All

ARTHURET CHURCH CHOIR BOYS AND REVD IVOR GRAHAM AT CROW WOOD ON THE GLEBE

stand in a ring in pairs, two in the middle. They chase one another round the ring, inside or out, until one stops in front of a pair, making three. The third must fly or be tigged. Tigger is relieved by tiggee. In tiggie-touchwood, so long as the child is touching wood he cannot be tigged. But he can be 'counted out.' In tiggie, 'we count out for the one who has to be *it*.'

Counting-out rhymes are connected with the 'Anglo-Cymric Score,' on which papers have appeared in these *Transactions* and elsewhere; and are the children's tradition of very ancient formularies. At Kirkoswald the verse runs:

> Eena meena mina mo,
> Vasaleena lina lo,
> A-way, flowery flock,
> (H)ellican pellican, ee wee,
> Wy wo wuss, – out goes she.

'Flower and flock,' or 'flowering flock,' are also used; and 'woss' for 'wuss.' At Clifton, near Penrith, they say:

> Eena meena mina mo,
> Basseleena lina lo,
> A-way, Kitty Macan,
> Who will be my serving-man
> To ride my horse and carry my gun?
> Tell me when my work is done.

> Ee, wee, wy wo wuss,
> Out goes she.

At Workington, *circa* 1850, the rhyme ran:

> Eena meena mina mo,
> Jack-a-lina slina slo,
> Kay way, Kitty Malan,
> Jack shall be my soldier man.
> O U T spells out:
> Hot scalding dish clout,
> You are right out.

Appleby has a shorter form, much debased:

> Eena meena mina mo,
> Catch a nigger by the toe,
> Hold him fast and don't let go,
> Eeena meena mina mo.

Another development is pretty well known. This is its form as it was used in Liverpool *circa* 1850:

> One-ery two-ery tickery teven,
> Allabo crackabo ten and eleven,
> Spink spang musky dann,
> Tweedlum twaddlum twenty-one,
> Black beaver, white trout,
> Eary ory, you are out.

'SETTLING SCORES AT YEARNGILL'

And at Kirkoswald they have a summary 'sentence of excommunication,' thus:

> Penny on the water,
> Tuppence on the sea,
> Thrippence on the railway,
> Out goes she.

The boys' games are without song, and are voiceless, except for the catches and calls. The girls' games are mostly played and danced to the accompaniement of songs and rhymes, which are always suitable and pleasing, and often very pretty. Some of these are too well known to need description; such are 'Nuts in May,' 'Buckets of water,' 'All around the village,' 'There was a jolly miller,' and 'Bingo'; 'Sally Walker,' the famous matrimonial game; 'Wall-flowers,' slightly varying from the form given in *English Folk-rhymes*, by G.F. Northall, p. 367, and Mr T.N. Postlethwaite's articles in the *North Lonsdale Magazine* (February and April, 1900); 'Robbers passing by,' also varying a little from Mr Postlethwaite's version; 'Here comes an old woman from Botany Bay,' the same as 'Old soldier' elsewhere; the wolf and sheep game, here called 'Jenny Lingo,' and played with expressive pantomime; 'How many miles to Barbary?' elsewhere 'to Babylon,' &c., about which it may be noted that at Workington it was formerly played on Good Friday evening, with 'Threed-a my needle, throp, throp, throp,' at the end of each verse.

BILLY BUMLEY HOUSE, WORKINGTON

HIGHFIELD, WORKINGTON

FLAG STREET, HAWKSHEAD

MONDAY AND TUESDAY

A game for ten girls. Seven sit or kneel on the floor. The mother counts over her seven children, and names them Monday, Tuesday, Wednesday, Thursday, Friday, Saturday, Sunday. She tells her servant, 'I am going out to [Carlisle]; roast one of the fattest children for dinner.' When she is gone, an old woman hidden behind a corner comes to the servant and says, 'May I have one of your children?' 'Yes, if you don't spit in my fireside.' She takes the fattest away. Presently the mother comes back, and says, 'Where is my dinner?' 'In the oven,' says the servant; but when she looks into the oven it is not there. Then she beats the servant. This goes on till all the children are taken away by the old woman. Then the mother returning and finding none of her children, goes up to the old woman, who is standing at the door, and says, 'Have you seen any of my children?' 'Yes,' says the old woman, 'I gave them each a penny, and set them to that man over there.' The mother goes to look for the children, cannot find them, and returning to the old woman tells her so. Then the old woman shouts, and all the children come running out and back to their mother.

Variant – An old *man* comes asking the servant, 'Please, can I get my pipe lit?' 'Yes, if you don't spit on the fender.' There are other variations of this game, which is very strange and obscure.

The Revd Canon Thornley, 'Transactions', C.& W.A.A.S.

LADY'S COTTAGE, CONISHEAD, ULVERSTON

CHAPEL ISLAND OR, AN ADVENTURE ON ULVERSTONE SANDS

The wills above be done! but I would fain die a dry death.

The Tempest

I have spent many a pleasant day at the village of Bardsea, three miles south of Ulverstone. . . . Bardsea is a pretty, out-of-the-way place; and the country about it is very picturesque. It is close to the sea, and commands a fine view of the bay, and of its opposite shores, for nearly forty miles. About a mile west of the village Birkrigg rises high above green pastures and leafy dells that lap his feet in beauty. Northward, the road to Ulverstone leads through the finest part of Conishead Park, which begins near the end of the village. This park is one of the most charming pieces of undulant woodland scenery I ever beheld. An old writer calls it 'the Paradise of Furness.'. . .

The last time I saw Bardsea it was about the middle of July. I had gone there to spend a day or two with a friend. There had not been a cloud on the heavens for a week; and the smell of new hay came on every sigh that stirred the leaves. The village looked like an island of sleepy life, with a sea of greenery around it, surging up to the doors of its white houses, and flinging the spray of nature's summer harmonies all over the place. . . . My friend and I wandered about from morning to night. In the heat of the day, the white roads glared in the sun; and, in some places, the air seemed to tremble, at about a man's height from the ground, as I have seen it tremble above a burning kiln sometimes. But, for broad day we had the velvet glades and shady woods of Conishead to ramble in; and many a rich old lane, and some green dells, where little brooks ran whimpling their tiny undersongs, in liquid trebles, between banks of wild flowers. Our evening walks were more delightful still; for when soft twilight came, melting the distinctions of the landscape in her dreamy loveliness, she had hardly time to draw 'a thin veil o'er the day' before sea and land began to shine again under the radiance of the moon. Wandering among such scenes, at such a time, was enough to touch any man's heart with gratitude for the privilege of existence in this world of ours.

My friend's house stands upon a buttressed shelf of land, half-way up the slope which leads from the shore into Bardsea. It is the most seaward dwelling of the place; and it is bowered about on three sides with little plots of garden, one of them kept as a playground for the children. It commands a glorious view of the bay, from Hampsfell, all round by Arnside and Lancaster, down to Fleetwood. Sometimes, at night, I have watched the revolutions of the Fleetwood light, from the front of the house, whilst listening to the surge of the tide along the shore, at the foot of the hill.

One day when dinner was over, we sat smoking at an open window, which looked out upon the bay. It was about the turning of the tide, for a fisherman's cart was coming slowly over the sands, from the nets at low water. The day was unusually hot; but, before we had smoked long, I felt as if I could't rest any longer in-doors.

'Where shall we go this afternoon?' said I, knocking the ashes out of my pipe upon the outside sill.

GREENODD SANDS

FOXFIELD

'Well,' replied my friend, 'I have been thinking that we couldn't do better than stroll into the park a while. What do you say?'

'Agreed,' said I. 'It's a fine piece of woodland. I daresay many a Roman soldier has been pleased with the place, as he marched through it, sixteen centuries ago.'

'Perhaps so,' said he, smiling, and taking his stick from the corner. 'Come along.'

At the garden gate we found three of his flaxen-headed children, romping with a short-legged Scotch terrier, called Trusty. The dog's wild eyes shone in little slits of dusky fire through the rusty thicket of gray hair which overhung them. Trusty was beside himself with joy when we came into the road; and he worried our shoes, and shook our trousers' slops in a sham fury, – as if they were imaginary rats; and he bounced about, and barked, till the quiet scene, from Bardsea to Birkrigg, rang with his noisy glee. Some of the birds about us seemed to stop singing for a few seconds, and, after they had taken an admiring look sideway at the little fellow, they burst out again, louder than ever, and in more rollicking strains, heartily infected with the frisky riot of that little four-legged marlocker. Both the dog and the children clamoured to go with us. My friend hesitated as first one, then another, tugged at him, and said: 'Pa, let me go.' Turning to me, he scratched his head, and said: 'I've a good mind to take Willie.' The lad instantly gave a twirl round on one heel, and clapped his hands, and then laid hold of his father's coatlap, by way of clenching the bargain at once. But just then his mother appeared at the gate, and said: 'Eh, no, Willie, you'd better not go. You'll be so tired. Come, stay with me. That's a good boy.' Willie let go his hold slowly, and fell back with a disappointed look. Trusty seemed to know that there was a hitch in the matter, for he suddenly became quieter; and, going up to Willie, he licked his hands consolingly, and then sitting down beside him, he looked round from one to another, to see how the thing was to end.

'Don't keep tea waiting for us,' said my friend; 'we'll be back in time for an early supper.'

'Very well,' replied his good-wife, 'we'll have something nice. Don't be late.'

The dog was now whining and wrestling in the arms of Willie, who was holding him back. We made our bows, and bade 'Good-bye' to the children and to their mother, and then turned up the road. Before we had gone many yards she called out, –

'I say, Chris; if you go as far as Ulverstone, call at Mrs Seatle's, and at Town and Fell's, for some things which I ordered. Bella Rigg can bring them down in her cart. These children want a new skipping rope, too; and you might bring something for Willie.' . . .

Once more we said 'Good-bye,' and walked up towards the white village; the chime of sweet voices sinking into a silvery hum as we got farther off. Everything in Bardsea was unusually still. Most of the doors and windows were open; and, now and then, somebody peeped out as we passed by, and said it was 'a fine day.' Turning round to look at the sands, we saw the dumpy figure of Owd 'Manuel, the fisherman, limping up from the foot of the slope, with his coat slung upon his arm. The old man stopped, and wiped his forehead, and gave his crutch a flourish, by way of salutation. We waved our hats, in reply, and went on. At the centre of the village stands the comfortable inn, kept by Old Gilly, the quaint veteran who, after spending the prime of manhood in hard service among the border smugglers, has settled down to close

MARKET STREET, ULVERSTON

GRAYRIGG SMITHY, KENDAL

the evening of his life in this retired nest. Here, too, all was still, except the measured sound of a shoemaker's hammer, ringing out from the open door of a cottage, where Cappel sat at his bench, beating time upon a leather sole, to the tune of a country song. And, on the shady side, next door to the yard wall, which partly encloses the front of the old inn, the ruddy, snow-capped face, and burly figure of Old Tweedler was visible, as still as statue. He was in his shirt sleeves, leaning against the door-cheek of his little grocery shop, smoking a long pipe, and looking dreamily at the sunny road. Tweedler needs a good deal of wakening at any time; but when he is once fairly wakened, he is a tolerable player on the clarionet, and not a very bad fiddler; and he likes to talk about his curious wanderings up and down the kingdom, with showfolk. . . .

There was not a sound of life in Old Gilly's house; but the trim cap of his kind dame was visible inside, bobbing to and fro by the window of the little bar. Gilly, in his kind-hearted way, always calls her 'Mammy.' We looked in at the bar, and the old lady gave us a cordial welcome. 'My good-man has just gone to lie down,' said she; 'but I'll go and tell him.' We begged that she would let him rest, and bring us three glasses of her best ale. The sun shone in strongly at the open back door. At the rear of the house, there is a shady verandah, and a garden in front of it. There we sat down, looking at the bright bay. The city of Lancaster was very distinct, on the opposite side of the water, more than twenty miles off. In a few minutes we heard Tweedler's carthorse tred, as he came through the lobby, with two books in his hand.

'There,' said he, handing one of them to me; 'I've turned that up amang a lot o' lummer i' th' house. I warnd it's just the thing for ye. What the devil is't, think ye? For it's past my skill.'

It was an old, well-thumbed, Latin Delectus, with one back off, and several leaves gone. It was not of much use to me; but when the old man said, 'Now, that's a fine book, I'll awarnd; an' I'll mak' ye a present on't,' I felt bound to receive it thankfully; and I did so.

'An' this,' said he, holding up the other; 'this is a book o' sangs. Cummerlan' sangs.'

It was a thin volume, in papered boards, – a cheap edition of Anderson's Ballads; printed in double column, royal octavo.

'Aye,' replied my friend; 'I should like to look at that.'

'Varra well,' said Tweedler; 'put it i' your pocket. I'll land it ye.' And then, as if half-repenting, he continued, 'But I set a deal o' store o' that book. I don't think as I could get another for ony money.'

'You shall have it back in a day or two,' said my friend.

'Oh,' replied Tweedler, 'it's all reight wi' ye. But I wouldn't ha' lant it onybody, mind ye.'

My friend put the book in his pocket, promising to take especial care of it; and then we drank up, and came away; and Tweedler sauntered back to lean against the door-cheek, and smoke.

It was about half-past one when we walked out at the landward end of the village. The only person we met was a horseman, riding hastily up from the skirt of the park. As he sped by, I recognised the tall figure and benevolent face of Dr

SHIP INN, SANDSIDE, MILNTHORPE

A—n, of Ulverstone. Near Bardsea Hall, an old lane leads off at the right-hand of the road, down to the sea-beach, from whence there is a pleasant walk along the shore of the Leven estuary, to a fishing village, called Sandside, and thence a good road, between rich meadow lands, up into Ulverstone. After a minute's conversation, at the end of this lane, we agreed to go that way. When we came out upon the shore, my friend stopped, and looked across the sands.

'Was you ever on Chapel Island?' said he, pointing towards it.

'No,' replied I; 'but I should like to see that spot. Is there any part of the old chantry left?'

'A little,' said he; 'mostly incorporated with the house of a fisherman who lives on the island. But we'll go over to it. There's nice time to get across before the tide comes in. It's not much more than a mile.'

I was pleased with the idea of seeing this little historic island, of which I had read and heard so much: so we strode out towards it at once. The sands between looked as level as a bowling-green, and perfectly dry; and it did not seem to me more than half the distance my friend had said. Before we had gone many yards he began a story:

'The last time I was on the island there were several friends – But hold! we had better take something to eat and drink. They'll have next to nothing there; and we shall have to stop till the next ebb. Wait here. I'll run back. I shan't be many minutes.' And away he went to the green lane.

SANDSIDE, KIRKBY-IN-FURNESS

KIRKBY-IN-FURNESS FROM THE SHORE

There was an old black boat on the sands, close to where he had left me. I got into it, and, pulling my hat over my eyes to shade the sun away, I lay down on my back and listened to the birds in Conishead Park. It was something more than a quarter of an hour before he appeared at the end of the lane again, with a brown bottle in one hand, and with pockets well stored. Without stopping an instant, he walked right out upon the sands, wiping the perspiration from his brow as he went. Staring straight at the island, he said, 'Come on. We've no time to lose, now. But we can manage it.' I remember fancying that there was an unusual earnestness in the tone of his voice; but I did not think much more about it at the time, for the sands still seemed quite dry between us and the island; so I followed him in silence, looking round at the beautiful scene, with my mind at ease. My friend was a tall, lithe man, in the prime of life; and a very good walker. I had not been well for some days previous, and I began to feel that the rate he was going at was rather too much for me. Besides, I had a pair of heavy, double-soled boots on, and my thick coat was loaded with books and papers. But I laboured on, perspiring freely. I thought that I could manage well enough to keep up with him for the distance we had to go. In a few minutes we began to come to patches of wet sand, where the feet sank at every step, and our progress was slower, and a good deal more difficult. We did not seem to get much nearer the island, though we were walking so hard. This tried me still more; and, not seeing any need for such a desperate hurry, I said, 'Don't go so fast!' But he kept up the pace, and, pointing to where a white sail was gliding up the other side of the island,

towards Ulverstone, he said, 'Come along! The main channel's filling! We've a channel to cross on this side, yet. D' ye see yon white line? It's the tide rushing in! Come on! We can't turn back now!' It was only then that I began to see how we were situated; and I tramped on at his heels, through the soft wet sand, perspiring and panting, and still without seeming to get over much ground. In a few minutes we came to a shallow channel, about eight or ten yards across. We splashed through, without speaking. It only took us a little above the knee; but I perceived that the water was rising rapidly. Thinking that the danger was over, I stammered out, 'Stop! Slacken a bit! We're all right now!' But the tone, as well as the words of his reply, startled me, as he shot ahead, crying, 'This is not it! This is nothing! Come on!' I was getting exhausted; and, when he cried out, 'Double!' and broke into a run, I had not breath to spare for an answer; but I struggled on desperately. The least false step would have brought me down; and, if I had fallen, I think that even that delay would have been more than we had to spare. Three or four minutes brought us up to the channel he had spoken of. It was an old bed of the river Leven. It must have been from fifteen to twenty yards wide at that moment, and the tide was increasing it at a terrible rate. When we got to the edge of the water, I was so done up that I panted out: 'Stop! I can't go so fast!' But my friend turned half round with a wild look, and almost screamed: 'But you *must*! It's death!' Then we went into the water, without any more words. I was a little on one side of him, and about two yards in the rear. It is a wonder to me now, how I got through that deep, strong, tidal current. The water must have revived me a little,

MR PRESTON AT SKELWITH FARM

unconsciously to myself, at the time. Before we had got to the middle, I saw the book of ballads which stuck up in the side pocket of my friend's shooting coat disappearing in the water as he went deeper into the channel. My clothes began to grow heavy, and the powerful action of the tide swayed me about so much that I could hardly keep my feet, and I expected every moment being whelmed over. But somehow I strove on, the water deepening at every step. A thousand thoughts crowded into my mind whilst wading that channel. I remember distinctly the terrible stillness of the scene; the frightful calm of the blue sky; the rocky island, with its little grove of trees waving gracefully in the sunshine – all so beautiful, yet all looking down with such a majestic indifference upon us, as we wrestled for life with the rising tide. About mid-channel, when the water was high up my breast, my friend gave a wild shout for help, and I instantly did the same. The nearest shore of the island was not much more than forty yards off. As my friend turned his head, I caught a glimpse of his haggard look, and I thought all was over. The rocks re-echoed our cries; but everything was still as death, except the little grove of trees waving in the sunshine. There was not a living soul in sight. My heart sank, and I remember feeling, for an instant, as if it was hardly worth while struggling any longer. And here let me bear testimony to a brave act on the part of my friend. In the deepest part of the channel, when the water was near the top of my shoulders, he put out his stick sideway, and said, 'Get hold!' I laid only a feeble grasp upon it, for I had enough to do to keep my feet. When we had waded about three yards in

this way, we began to see that we were ascending the opposite bank rapidly, for it was steeper than the other one. In two minutes more we were out upon the dry sands, with our clothes clinging heavily about us, and our hearts beating wild with mingled emotions. 'Now,' said I, panting for breath, 'let's sit down a minute.' 'No, no!' replied he in a resolute tone, pushing on; 'Come farther off.' A walk of about thirty yards brought us to the foot of the rocks. We clambered painfully up from stone to stone, till we came upon a little footpath which led through the grove and along the garden to the old fisherman's cottage, on the north side of the island. As we entered the grove I found that my friend had kept hold of the brown bottle all the way. I did not notice this till we came to the first patch of grassy ground, where he flung the bottle down and walked on in silence, panting for breath. He told me afterwards that he believed it had helped to steady him whilst coming through the channel.

The fisherman's cottage is the only dwelling on the little island. We found the door open; and the birds were singing merrily among the green bushes about the entrance. There was nobody in but the old fisherman's wife, and she was deaf. We might have shouted long enough before she could have heard us; and if she had heard, the poor old body could hardly have helped us. When we got to the door she was busy with something at the fire, and she did not hear our approach. But, turning round, and seeing us standing there, she gazed a few seconds with a frightened look, and then lifting up both hands, she cried out, 'Eh, dear o' me, good folk? Whativver's

CARTMEL PRIORY

to do? Whereivver han yo cam fra? Eh; heawivver han yo getten ower?'

We told our tale in a few words; and then she began again:

'Good lorjus days, childer! What browt yo through t' channel at sich an ill time as this? It's a marcy 'at yo weren't draan'd mony a time ower! It mud ha' bin my awn lads! Eh, what trouble there'd ha' bin, for someb'dy. What, ye'll ha' mothers livin', likely; happen wives and childer? . . . Eh, dear o' me! Bud cum in wi' ye! Whativver are ye stonnin' theer for? Cum in; an get your claes off, – do! An' get into bed, this minute,' said she, pointing to a little, low-roofed room in the oldest part of the house.

The water from our clothes was running over the floor; but when we spoke about it in the way of apology, the old woman said, 'Nivver ye mind t' watter. Ye've had watter enough for yance, I should think. Get in theer, I tell ye; an' tak your weet claes off. Now, don't stan' gabblin; but creep into bed, like good lads; an' I'll bring ye some het tea to drink. . . . Eh, but ye owt to be thankful 'at ye are wheer ye are! . . . Ye'd better go into that inside room. It'll be quieter. Leave your claes i' this nar room, an' I'll hing 'em up to dry. An' put some o' thoose aad shirts on. They're poor, but they're comfortable. Now, in wi' ye! Ye can talk at efter. . . . Eh; the Lord help us! It's a grate marcy! It's a grate marcy!'

The old woman had four grown-up sons, labourers and fishermen; and there was plenty of working clothes belonging to them, lying about the two bedrooms. After we had stript our wet things, and flung them down, one after another, with a splash, we put on a rough shirt apiece, and crept into bed. In a few minutes she came in with a quart pitcher full of hot tea, and a cup to drink it from; and setting it down upon a chair at the bedside, she said, 'Now; get that into ye; an' hev a bit ov a sleep.'

We lay still, talking and looking about us; but we could not sleep. The excitement we had gone through had left a band of intense pain across the lower part of my forehead, as if a hot wire was burning into it. The walls of the room we lay in were partly those of the ancient chapel which gives its name to the island. In fact, the little ragged weed-grown belfry still stood above our heads, almost the only relic of the ruined chantry, except the foundations, and some pieces of the old walls built up into the cottage. This chapel was founded above five centuries ago, by the monks of Furness. Here they prayed daily 'for the safety of the souls of such as crossed the sands with the morning tide.' The Priory of Conishead was charged with the maintenance of guides across this estuary, which is perhaps the most dangerous part of the Morecambe Sands. . . . I can imagine how solemn the pealing of that little island

NATLAND CHURCH, NEAR KENDAL

chapel's bell must have sounded upon the shores of the estuary, floating over those dangerous waters its daily warning of the uncertainty of human life. Perhaps the bodies of drowned men might have lain where we were lying; or travellers, rescued from the tide by those ancient ministers of religion, might have listened with grateful hearts to the prayers and thanksgivings offered up in that venerable chantry. The chastening interest of old pious usage clings to the little island still; and it stands in the midst of the waters, preaching in mute eleoquence to every thoughtful mind. There was something in the sacred associations of the place; there was something in the mouldering remnant of the little chapel, which helped to deepen the interest of our eventful visit that day. We could not sleep. The sun shone in aslant at the one tiny window of our bedroom, and the birds were singing merrily outside. As we lay there, thinking and talking about these things, my friend said, 'I feel thankful now that, I did not bring Willie with me. If I had done so, nothing could have saved us.' The tide had come in behind, and a minute more at the channel would have been too much.

After resting about three hours we got up, and put on some of the cast-off clothes which had been worn by the old woman's sons whilst working in the land. My trousers were a good deal too long, and they were so stiff with dried slutch that they almost stood up of themselves. When they were on, I felt as if I was dressed in sheet-iron. I never saw two stranger figures than we cut that day, as we entered the kitchen again, each amusing himself with the other's comical appearance.

'Never ye mind,' said the old woman; 'there's naabody to see ye bud mysel; ye may think varra weel 'at ye're alive to wear owt at all. But sart'ny ye looken two bonny baygles! I daat varra mich whether your awn folk would knaw ye. It quite alters your fayturs. I shouldn't tak ye to be aboon ninepence to t' shillin', at the varra most. As for ye,' said she, addressing myself; 'ye'n na 'casion to talk; for ye're as complate a flay-crow as ivver I set een on.'

The kitchen was cleaned up, and the things emptied from our pockets lay about. Here books and papers were opened out to dry. There stockings hung upon a line; and our boots were reared against the fender, and their soles turned to the fire. On the dresser two little piles of money stood, and on a round table were the sandwiches and hard-boiled eggs which my friend had brought in his pockets.

'What are ye for wi' this?' said the old woman, pointing to the eatables. 'One or two o't eggs are crushed a bit, but t' ham's naa warse, 'at I can see.'

'Let us taste what it is like,' said my friend.

'That's reight,' replied she; 'an' ye'll hev a cup o' het tea to it. I have it ready here.'

The tea was very refreshing; but we couldn't eat much, for we had not quite recovered from the late excitement. After a little meal, we went out to walk upon the island. Our damp clothes were fluttering upon the green bushes about the cottage. They were drying fast; for, though the sun was hot, a cool breeze swept over the bay from the south-west. We wandered through the grove, and about the garden, or rather the 'kail-yard,' for the chief things grown in it were potatoes, cabbages, broccoli, pot-herbs, and such like things, useful at dinner time. There were very few flowers in it, and they were chiefly such as had to take care of themselves. In the grove,

DERWENT BAY, KESWICK

there were little bowery nooks, and meandering footpaths, mostly worn by visitors from the neighbouring shores. The island has been much larger than it is now. Great quantities of limestone rock have been sold, and carried away to the mainland; and it seems as if this little interesting leaf of local history was fated to ultimate destruction in that way. We walked all round it, and then we settled down upon a grassy spot, at the south-western edge, overlooking the channel we had waded through. There was something solemn in the thought, that instead of gazing upon the beautiful bay, we might have been lying at that moment in the bed of the channel there, with the sunny waters rippling above us, or drifting out with the retiring tide to an uncrowded grave in the western sea. The thick woods of Conishead looked beautiful on the opposite shore, with the white turrets of the Priory rising out of their embowering shades. A little south of that the spire of Bardsea church pointed heavenward from the summit of a green hill, marking the spot where the village stood hidden from our view. White sails were gliding to and fro upon the broad bay, like great swans with sunlit wings. It was a beautiful scene. We sat looking at it till we began to feel chill, and then we went back to the cottage.

About six o'clock the old fisherman returned home from Ulverstone; and, soon after, two of his sons arrived from Conishead Park, where they had been working at a deep drain. They were tall, hardy-looking men, about middle age. The old fisherman, who knows the soundings of the sands all round, seemed to think we had picked our way to the island as foolishly as it was possible to do. He talked about the matter as if we had as good a knowledge of the sands as himself, and had set out with the express intention of doing a dangerous exploit.

'Now,' said he, pointing a good way north of the track we had taken, 'if ye'd ha' come o'er by theer, ye mud ha' done it easy. Bud, what the devil, ye took the varra warst nook o' th' channel. *I* wonder as ye weren't *draan'd*. I've helped to get mony a ane aat o' that hole, — baith deead an' alive. I yence pulled a captain aat by th' yure o' th' yed, as had sailed all ower th' warld, nearly. An' we'd summat to do to bring him raand, an' all. He was that far geean. . . . Now, if ye'd ha' getten upo' yon bank,' continued he, 'ye mud ha' managed to ha' studden till help had come to ye. What, ye wadn't ha' bin varra mich aboon t' middle. . . . But it's getten near law watter. I mun be off to t' nets. Will ye go daan wi' me?'

BOATING AT GRASMERE

There were two sets of 'stake nets' belonging to the island; one on the north end, and the other on the western side, in our own memorable channel. The sons went to those on the north; and the old man took a stick in his hand, and a large basket on his arm, and we followed him down the rocks to the other nets. They are great cages of strong net-work, supported by lofty poles, or stakes, from which they take their name. They are so contrived that the fish can get into them at high water, but cannot escape with the retiring tide. There was rather more than a foot of water at the bottom of the nets; but there was not a fish visible, till the old man stepped in; and then I saw that flukes lay thick about the bottom, half-hidden in the sand. We waded in, and helped to pick them up, till the great basket was about half full. He then closed the net, and came away, complaining that it was 'nobbut a poor catch.' When we got to the cottage, we put on our own clothes, which were quite dry. And, after we had picked out two dozen of the finest flukes, which the old man strung upon a stout cord for ease of carriage, we bade adieu to the fisherman and his family, and we walked away over the sands, nearly by the way we had come to the island. . . . When we drew near my friend's house, he said, 'Now, we had better not mention this little affair to our people.' But, as we sat at supper that night, I could not help feeling thankful that we were eating fish, instead of being eaten by them.

Edwin Waugh

CHAR-FISHING

No account of fishing in the English Lake District at the present time would be quite complete without some mention of Char. A separate description is necessary, because these fish seldom rise to a fly, and, when they are not netted, are usually caught by Trolling, which is differently managed at different times of the year.

The Plumb-line – Early in the season, that is to say in the end of March and during April and the first weeks of May, the Char are found very deep, in about ninety feet of water. It is necessary then to use the plumb-line, though difficult to manage.

You have about 40 yards of strong fine line, six-thread, with a pound and a half of lead, pear-shaped, at the end. The plumb has sometimes a wing or fin of tin inserted to prevent its spinning and twisting the line. To this plumb-line you attach at different depths half a dozen gut lines, with 3 or 4 swivels on each; they should be of salmon gut, as they have occasionally to bear very considerable strain. The lowest gut line is about three yards long; the highest about five. In this way you will be sure to hit the right depth for the fish.

John Beever

HIGHGATE, KENDAL

FLY-RODS AND LANDING-NETS

Mr Beever's model was excellent, no doubt; but nowadays fly-rods are made more or less with Hickory, Green-heart, or Split-cane; and the tops are sometimes Lancewood. They are brought to such perfection, with balance-handles, snake-rings, and lock-joints, that it is hardly worth while to go to the trouble and expense of making a rod at home. The number of joints is a matter of taste: more than three are not necessary. As a rule, however, every fisherman has his own pet rod, and will hear of no other.

A landing-net should be carried, if there is a chance of a big fish. A very good model, which can be used while wading, has a short handle, a pear-shaped ash ring, water-proof net, and a clip which fixes on to the strap of the basket. This net can be brought into action very easily, and is quite as serviceable as more elaborate patterns.

John Beever

PRACTICAL FLY FISHING

It may be necessary to say that the hooks are the Kendal ones; numbering from 00 to 16 – the double cypher being the smallest Trout, and No. 16 the largest Salmon hook. A hook exceeding No. 6 is rarely used for Trout flies.

These hooks, which are excellent in quality and reasonable in price, are made by Mr Philip Hutchinson,· late partner of, and successor to, the famous Adlington, of Kendal; and I think that they are now made better, and more equal in temper, than I ever remember them to have been.

Mr Hutchinson is very obliging in making hooks to order, of any kind which the angler thinks more suitable than the regular sorts for any particular purpose. I had a few hundred bright ones, made by him some years ago, and they answered well for fly-fishing on bright sunny days. Of course the size of hook and fly varies with the *water*. For instance, if No. 2 is mentioned, an average water is meant. No. 3 would be the same fly for a high and No. 1 for a low water.

·*Whose successors, Messrs G. Hutchinson & Co., of 43 Stricklandgate, Kendal, worthily sustain the reputation of the house.*

John Beever

97

LONGTOWN SCHOOLCHILDREN WITH MR BLACK (THE HEADMASTER)

CASTERTON: SCHOOLS

The Clergy Daughters' School was founded in 1823 by the Revd William Carus Wilson M.A. perpetual curate of Casterton from 1833, & first established at Cowen Bridge, but removed here in 1833; it has an endowment of £6,165 in Consols, given by deed in 1834, & now (1897) producing about £185 a year; the school is available for 112 girls, & there are at present 108. Attached is a sanatorium, built in 1878; Charlotte Brontë, the distinguished novelist, was a pupil at the school when it was carried on at Cowen Bridge, and has severely satirized both the school and its founder in her 'Jane Eyre.' Miss Mabel Williams, of Newnham College, Cambridge, mistress.

Low Wood Middle Class Boarding School for Girls has an attached sanatorium, built in 1883; the school is controlled by a body of trustees; the Ven. Archdeacon Cooper, chairman; the Right Revd Henry Ware D.D. treasurer; Revd A.D. Burton M.A. sec.; Miss Sarah Daniels, lady superintendent.

Kelly's Directory, 1897

ANNIE HODGSON AND ELIZABETH FARREL OF LONGTOWN

BUILDING THE TRAMWAY, THE COURTS ON THE CRESCENT, CARLISLE

CARLISLE

The city is well-built, and has two main thoroughfares, striking out from the market place, as in most cities of Roman origin, and from these diverge a number of smaller streets. The Caldew is crossed by three stone bridges, erected in 1820, and the Nelson bridge, built in 1852. Another of white freestone, designed by Mr R. Smirke, jun. and constructed in 1872, at a cost of about £70,000, spans the Eden; it consists of five elliptical arches and is connected with the town by an arched causeway; another, of three arches, crosses the Petteril; the rivers all abound with fish.

The water works were acquired by the Corporation in 1866 from a local company. The supply, obtained from the river Eden, is filtered at Stoneyholme and afterwards pumped into a distributing reservoir at Harraby Hill and thence flows by gravitation through the town.

The Gas works, which adjoin the Victoria viaduct were similarly acquired by the Corporation in 1850. Extensions were made in 1894, and for the purpose six acres of ground, purchased at Boustead's grassing.

The Citadel passenger railway station, in Court square, is a noble pile of buildings of white stone, in the Decorated Gothic style, and receives the traffic of seven different lines, viz: the Caledonian, Glasgow and South Western, London and North Western, Maryport and Carlisle, Midland, North British and Silloth and Port Carlisle, Amalgamated and North Eastern, and is thus a great railway centre, being the point of divergence of lines to North and West Cumberland, and to the North East of England, as well as the first important stopping place after leaving Scotland, by the North British and Caledonian lines. The original station, built in 1847, was provided with a single line only, this being also used for goods traffic. In 1861 the station was lengthened and the goods traffic diverted behind the outer wall. During the period 1873–76 the station, which is about 440 yards long by 120 wide, was enlarged to its present dimensions, the island platforms and buildings thereon erected, and an approach made to the same from the Victoria viaduct, which had been erected contemporaneously; and the goods traffic was then removed from the station and carried on by new lines laid through Long Island and Denton-Holme. The station with its approaches covers an area of about 13 acres. It is the property of the L. & N. W. & Caledonian Railway companies, and is managed by a joint committee. It is estimated that from 200 to 250 trains leave here daily.

CARLISLE CITADEL STATION IN THE 1890s

CARLISLE STATION, 1910

CARLISLE

The Victoria viaduct, opened on Thursday, Sept. 20, 1877, by H.R.H. the Princess Louise, comprises the whole of the line of road, then newly laid out, from English street to the river Caldew; the total length of the viaduct proper being about 880 yards, and the width throughout 45 feet. The work was carried out in part by the London and North Western and Caledonian Railway companies, who contributed jointly the sum of £38,000, and partly by the Corporation, and occupied about two years; the plans were prepared by Mr George M. Cunningham C.E. of Edinburgh, and Mr S.B. Worthington C.E. of Manchester, in consultation with the city surveyor, and had the general supervision of the Improvement Committee of the Town Council.

Carlisle was formerly an inland port, communicating with the Solway Firth at Bowness, by means of a canal 11 miles in length, begun in 1819, and completed in 1823 at a cost of about £90,000, and navigable for vessels of 100 tons burthen. This canal is now abolished, and its bed has been utilised for the laying down of a line of railway to Port Carlisle, in connection with the North British system, but owing to the obstruction caused by the viaduct of the Caledonian Railway Co. which crosses the Solway some distance below, only very small vessels are able to reach the port, and the traffic is therefore diverted to Silloth, 22 miles distant, which is now the actual port for Carlisle. The line and docks at Port Carlisle are the property of the North British Railway Co.

Kelly's Directory, 1897

HOTELS AND TARIFFS

Abbreviations: R., bed-room; S.R., private sitting-room; b., breakfast; l., lunch; t., tea; d., dinner; a., attendance; fr., from.

AMBLESIDE

Taylor's Salutation, Queen's and **Waterhead:** R., 2/- to 5/-; S.R., 3/6 to 7/6; b., 2/- to 3/-; l., 2/- to 3/-; t., 1/6 to 3/-; d., 3/6 to 5/-.

Low Wood: R., 2/6 to 6/6; S.R., 6/- to 10/6; b., 2/6 ; l., 2/-; t., 9d.; d., 5/-; a., 1/6. Pension, 10/- to 12/- per day.

Skelwith Hotel, Skelwith Bridge: *Pension*, 7/- each per week for small party; 6/- for large party. S.R., 21/- per week extra for party of less than six.

BOWNESS

Rigg's Crown: R.,from 4/-; b., 1/6, 2/-, 2/6; l., from 2/-; t., from 1/-; d., 4/6; S.R., 5/-. Pension, from 10/6 per day; 70/- per week (to end of July).

New Ferry: R., 3/- to 5/-; S.R., 4/- to 7/6; b., 2/6 to 3/-; l., 2/6; t., 1/-; d., 4/6; a., 1/6.

Old England: R., 2/6; b., 2/6; l., 2/6; t., 1/-; d., 5/-; a., 1/6. Pension, 12/- per day; 63/- per week.

Royal Oak: R., 2/-; b., 1/6; l., 1/6; d., 2/-.

GRASMERE

Prince of Wales and Rothay: R., 2/6; S.R., 4/- to 10/6; b., 1/6 to 2/6; l., 2/- to 3/-; t., 1/- to 2/6; d., 3/- to 4/-; a., 1/6 (Whitsuntide to September 30th).

Pearson's Gossipy Guide to the English Lakes

AMBLESIDE CENTRE

PRINCE OF WALES, GRASMERE

PONY RIDE AT THE PRINCE OF WALES, GRASMERE

ADVERTISING

Support English Trade and Buy English made Pencils.

ESTABLISHED 1832. ROYAL PATRONAGE.
Prize Medals: London, 1851 & 1862; Paris, 1867.
BY APPOINTMENT
TO ALL HIS MAJESTY'S GOVERNMENT OFFICES.
—
THE KESWICK PENCIL WORKS.
—
HOGARTH & HAYES
(*Successors to A. Wren, Guy, & Co., and Ann Banks*),
*BLACK LEAD PENCIL
AND CEDAR GOODS . .
MANUFACTURERS, . .*
SOUTHEY HILL, KESWICK.

Visitors may spend a very enjoyable and instructive visit to this Establishment, where the interesting process of Pencil Making may be witnessed in all its branches. Last season the Princess Victoria of Wales and the Duchess of York, &c., &c., visited the works, and expressed their admiration at the manner in which the Pencils are made.

Pearson's Gossipy Guide to the English Lakes

TEA AT DALTON HALL, BURTON-IN-KENDAL

LODORE HOTEL, KESWICK

ON SOME SURVIVING FAIRIES

Read at Carlisle, June 20th, 1900

The shyness of the British fairy in modern times has given rise to a widespread belief that the whole genus must be regarded as extinct. No doubt the great increase of the three R's, which are the natural enemies of fairies, has driven them to take refuge in the least accessible neighbourhoods; but occasional specimens are still to be obtained. The injudicious collector who hunts, so to say, with horn and hounds, will draw every cover blank; and even the aids to scouting formulated in folklore tracts may not always insure success. We have, however, found two or three living examples which I now exhibit, only withholding the precise *habitat*, as in the case of some rare ferns, which botanists are quite justified in protecting from the dangers of too fierce a light of publicity. Fairies, it is well known, thrive only in moonshine.

Of a certain place I had heard, many years back, that it was haunted, but without further details.

Lately we got the following information from a trustworthy source:

'There used to be fairies at the spot, before the wood was cut down . . .'

Where was the wood?

'It was on the top of the Bank,' – where now no trace of it remains.

'Well; they went away when it was cut down; but once they set some Fairy Butter ready for a ploughman, when he was going to have his dinner. One of his horses ate it; the other did not. The one that did not eat it died. They used to be in the cottage yonder, that is now a cow-shed. It's lucky,' added the old man, 'if you eat fairy butter.'

The exact nature of the article is described in the late Canon Atkinson's *Forty Years in a Moorland Parish*, and it used to be a well-known commodity in the North of England.

The next story is told in the same neighbourhood:

'There was a fairy that looked like a hare. *It was a real fairy*, but a man caught it for a hare, and put it in a bag, and thought he would have a nice Sunday dinner. While it was in the bag it saw its father outside, and he called to it "Pork, pork!" and it cried out "Let me go to daddy!" And then the man was angry, and said "Thoo ga to thy daddy!" and it went away to its daddy; and he was very much disappointed at not getting his Sunday dinner.'

The same authority told another tale of a house just beyond the eastern border of Cumberland, mentioned as a haunt of the common Brownie or Hobthrush:

'Once there was a little fairy and it lived at a farmhouse in — that used to do all the work before they were down in

104

CROSBY RAVENSWORTH

the morning; and so they found out about it, and they got up one morning to see it, and they saw a little fairy running across the yard. It had a green jacket and a little hood and a red skirt, and they thought it looked very ragged, and they got it a new suit of clothes and put them in the kitchen where it would be most likely to come to. And so it saw them in the morning, and it said:

> A new coat, a new hood!
> Now little Hobberst will do no more good!

And it never came back any more, and they *were* sorry when they lost the little fairy; and they called it Little Hobberst. It would sup porridge if they were set out for it, though it would not have the clothes.'

Mrs Hodgson, Transactions, C. & W.A.A.S.

OLD PUMP INN, KENDAL

'FIRST FOOT'

The superstition concerning 'first-foot' has not yet died out; but the observance is not regarded with that seriousness which ruled half a century ago, and to the next generation, probably, this ancient New Year's custom and belief will have become part of the history of the bygone.

Daniel Scott

BRITANNIA FIRES JUBILEE SALUTE, 1897, WINDERMERE

CYCLING

A friend of ours who was taking his bicycle on board a Windermere steamer was thus rebuked by one of the sailors with typical northern bluntness: 'I can't imagine,' grumbled this very candid person, 'why people want to take their bicycles by boat, when they've got the best roads to cycle on anywhere in England.'

Now we agree that the roads in parts of the district would be difficult to beat, though they are apt after even moderate rain to become unpleasantly greasy. Lest anyone, however, should come down to Westmorland with the idea that the country can be properly explored on a bicycle, it may be as well to make a few points clear.

The roads in what may be called the sub-alpine region – the region lying outside the bigger hills – have generally as good a surface as could be desired, though they are naturally exceedingly hilly. Only two decent roads, however, penetrate the mountains from side to side. The first of these runs from Windermere to Keswick by Ambleside, Grasmere, and Thirlmere – where there is a loop on the western side of the lake; the second from Windermere – with a branch up from Ambleside – over the top of the Kirkstone, down Patterdale, and by the northern shore of Ullswater to Penrith. These roads are magnificent throughout; and though, of course, it is, from any side, a tremendous push up the Kirkstone, the road – though liable, no doubt, to be torn up by storms – is sometimes as smooth as a billiard table. Dunmail Raise, on the other route, will be considered a mere trifle.

These, however, are the only two good roads which traverse the whole breadth of the district. Other lanes, with excellent

TOP OF HONISTER

SPARK BRIDGE

surface, penetrate far into the mountain valleys; but they then degenerate into impossible tracks, as the roads over Wrynose and Honister Hause, or end altogether in mere *culs-de-sac*, as at Mardale, Langdale, and Wastdale Heads, or at the end of Borrowdale. It is, of course, possible to push a bicycle over Honister or Wrynose – we have toiled with one over the latter ourselves but to call such work cycling would be foolish.

It is competent, accordingly, for the cyclist who does not mind sometimes retracing his steps – if the expression may pass – to explore the bottoms of most of the valleys; he is debarred from wandering on from dale to dale over the ruggeder mountain passes. The noble track, for instance, from Buttermere to Langdale over Scarf Gap, Black Sail, and Esk Hause, is wholly beyond his reach. Yet it is only by taking some track like this that one gets properly to know the *arcana* of the district.

So the matter may be summed up thus. For those who are staying at this or that centre, a bicycle is a useful accessory; for those who are bent on a progressive tour, moving on continually from sleeping-place to sleeping-place, it is merely an annoying encumbrance. Those who do cycle should always have good brakes, and should remember that many of the more dangerous and out-of-the-way hills have no C.T.C. warning boards, *and are constantly crossed by unexpected gates.* We have frequently drawn attention to dangerous descents, *but no conclusion must be drawn from, or reliance placed on, our silence.*

Pearson's Gossipy Guide to the English Lakes

IN THE DERWENT, NEAR KESWICK

ST LUKE'S FAIR, KIRKBY STEPHEN

FAIRS & MARKETS – WESTMORLAND

Ambleside, market day, wed.; fairs, Whit Wednesday & October 29 for cattle & October 13 for sheep

Appleby, market day, sat.; fairs, St Lawrence's day, August 21; Whit Monday; Martinmas & a great fair on the second tues. wed. & thurs. in June

Brough, fairs on September 30 & October 1 for woollen cloth & other merchandise & for sheep, horses & cattle & on the second thurs. in January, February, March & April for cattle & sheep

Burton-in-Kendal, fair on Easter Monday for cattle & sheep

Kendal, market day, sat.; fairs, February 22 for horses; March 22, April 29 & November 8 for cattle; Whit Saturday & Martinmas for hiring servants; on November 9 for horses & on every alternate mon for fat sheep & cattle

Kirkby Lonsdale, market day, Thursday; fairs, April 5, for cattle & cloth; 5 October for cattle & horses & 21 December for cattle; other cattle fairs are held on Holy Thursday & St Thomas' day & one three weeks after Holy Thursday

Kirkby Stephen, market day, mon.; fairs, 29 September & 29 October & hiring fairs on the last monday in June & first monday in July

Milnthorpe, market day, fri.; fairs on 12 May & 17 October

Orton, market day, wed.; fairs for cattle on 3 May & the fri. before Whitsuntide & on the second fri. following is a fair for earthenware; on August 20 for sheep & on the first fri. after Michaelmas day is a cattle & pleasure fair

Shap, market day, mon.; fairs, 4 May & 23 September, for cattle, sheep & merchandise

Staveley, fair, 7 October for sheep & cattle

Kelly's Directory, 1897

KIRKBY STEPHEN ST LUKE'S FAIR

In 1890 'Luke Fair' was described as: 'this dirty, noisy and rough old fair, dedicated to the memory of mutton, has come and gone and left its trail of dirt behind it. The town was turned into a huge camp for the space of two days, and drinking booths, not nearly in such numbers as formerly, lined the streets. The Proclamation was read from the "Charterstone," near the New Oddfellows Hall, but the bustling crowd of buyers and sellers was sadly oblivious of the ceremony, and went on its way with a smile at the relic of a bye-gone age.'

The number of sheep exposed in pens, erected by the inhabitants and let to the owners of sheep, at the fair in 1909 was estimated at 20,000, and the prices 5/- or more per head down. Blackfaced lambs 7/- to 15/-; wethers, two and three years old, 17/- to 22/-; ewes 12/- to 24/-; tups £1 to £5; greyfaced lambs 14/- to 26/-; shearlings 26/- to 32/-; ewes to 35/-; Wensleydale tups £2 to £5; bullock calves £5 to £6; strong bullocks £9 to £11.

F. W. Garnett

AMBLESIDE RUSHBEARING

GRASMERE RUSHBEARING

WESLEYAN CHAPEL, SHAP

MARDALE

Mardale is a chapelry and mountainous township, mostly in the parish of Shap, but partly in Bampton parish, 5 miles south-west from Shap station on the London and North Western railway, 5½ south-west from Bampton, 9½ west from Shap by road and 6 across the mountains through Swindale, and 15 south from Penrith, near the end of a deep, fertile and beautifully picturesque valley, encompassed by lofty mountains and fells, in the Northern division of the county, West Ward division and union, petty sessional division of West Ward, county court district of Penrith, rural deanery of Lowther and archdeaconry and diocese of Carlisle. The church is a small and plain building of stone, with a low square tower containing one bell, and affords 70 sittings. The registers date from the year 1684. The living is a vicarage net yearly value £131, in the gift of the vicar of Shap, and held since 1894 by the Revd William Terry L.Th. of Durham University. About a mile down the valley is the head of Hawes Water, a beautiful lake in the manor of Thornthwaite and in the parishes of Mardale and Shap; it is 3 miles in length and from a quarter to half-a-mile wide, sheltered on the east by the steep and well-wooded rocks of Naddle forest, descending to the water's edge; on the western side there is a good road and a few farmhouses, and

cultivated fields extend for some distance up the mountain sides, the lake receives the Measand beck on the west, and the Randale and Riggindale becks at its southern extremity; and a beck flowing out of it on the north falls into the river Lowther at Brampton; the mountains enclosing its southern half include High Raise Whelter (2,634 feet), Kidsty Pike (2,560 feet), and High Street (2,700 feet), which takes its name from an ancient Roman road on the top, running southwards from Penrith; it is now covered with green sward, and is supposed to be the highest road in England. Another grand peak is Harter Fell, between which and Branstreet (2,333 feet) is Gatesgarth pass. The lake is the property of the Earl of Lonsdale, and permission for boating or fishing must be applied for at Lowther Castle. Near Haweswater are some long mounds, or barrows, known as 'The Giants' graves.' About 2 miles south of the lake are two small tarns called 'Bleawater' and 'Smallwater,' and further south, through the Nan Bield pass, is the Kentmere reservoir. A short distance beyond the chapel at Greenhead is the Dun Bull inn, a homely but comfortable house for visitors. The Earl of Lonsdale is lord of the manor and principal landowner. The soil is loam and very fertile in the valley, affording excellent pasturage. The area is 2,214 acres.

Kelly's Directory, 1897

KENDAL HOSPITAL

PLUMGARTHS HYDROPATHIC ESTABLISHMENT

PLUMGARTHS ESTABLISHMENT is in one of the most picturesque and healthy parts of the Kingdom; within two miles of Kendal, six of Windermere, and seven of the warm and sandy shores of Morecame Bay. Situated on the sunny breast of a pastoral slope, looking down on the rich Vale of the River Kent, and visited alternately by the finely-tempered breezes of sea and mountain, its atmosphere is peculiarly pure and invigorating; while there is the advantage of easy access to the Lakes, with the additional one of being sufficiently removed from their humid exhalations.

The internal accommodations and comforts at Plumgarths are those of a genuine English Home, making it suitable as a Resort in all parts of the year; there is an efficient supply of Water, cold or warm, for Treatment carefully and scientifically adapted to each case; and a Dietary as liberal and varied as the laws of health will permit. Extensive Recreation Grounds command magnificent Views of the Westmorland, Cumberland, Lancashire, and Yorkshire Mountains; and cheerful Walks, Rides, and Resting-places abound in every direction.

The Bath-rooms (one of which is within the House) are fitted up with every variety of Hydrotherapeutic Apparatus; there is also Portable Apparatus for each Bed-room; a Turkish-bath has been constructed for such Patients as are likely to benefit by its occasional use; quiet and agreeable domestic pastimes are encouraged; and everything promotive of calm enjoyment and speedy restoration is constantly kept in view.

Arrivals are met with a suitable Conveyance at the Kendal Railway Station, or at Windermere or Burneside, by pre-arrangement, and a special Post-bag (*via* Kendal) arriving at the Establishment every morning by Seven o'clock, is despatched in the evening at Half-past Eight.

TERMS FOR BOARD AND LODGING, WITH ADVICE AND TREATMENT:

Patients occupying First-class Bed-rooms 2 15 0 per Week.
   "   "   Second Bed-rooms 2 2 0   "
Two persons occupying one Bedroom, Guests not under Treatment, or Patients coming in for Treatment only, proportionably less.

Address – DR SPENCER HALL,
PLUMGARTHS ESTABLISHMENT, KENDAL.

Prospectus for Plumgarths, Kendal

THE LAKE COUNTIES

Skiddaw has a claim upon us as one of the first mountains that tempted climbers for the sake of the scenery. There had been travellers and explorers, hermits and hunters before; but I do not think it often happened that people went up to the heights for the mere pleasure of going there. Bishop Nicolson, in his diary for May 20, 1684, records that he went up Skiddaw with some friends, and about this time it seems to have been a well-known point of view. Housman, who tells the story of his climb in 1798 which he 'inconsiderately undertook to perform without a guide,' says that towards the northern extremity of the summit of 'this stupendous mountain' where 'chasms of enormous depths in the bowels of the mountains, forming steeps of slaty shiver, yawn upwards with frightful grin, and threaten to swallow inferior hills,' there were ruins of a hut. 'It is said,' he continues, 'that this building was made in 1689 by Mr John Adams, the geographer, of a sufficient size to contain his telescopes and optic glasses, whereby he was enabled to give a better description of the two counties; but being arrested by his engraver, and death soon following, his labours were lost.' But by Housman's time there was already a

track to the top; Mrs Radcliffe, who wrote 'The Mysteries of Udolpho,' had published her account of the great adventure. She began by saying, 'We stood on a pinnacle, commanding the whole dome of the sky,' and concluded, 'The air on this summit was boisterous, intensely cold, and difficult to be inspired, though the day was, below, warm and serene. It was dreadful to look down from nearly the brink of the point on which we stood upon the lake of Bassenthwaite, and over a sharp and separated ridge of rocks, that from below appeared of a tremendous height, but now seemed not to reach half-way up Skiddaw; it was almost as if

> "the precipitation might down stretch
> Below the beam of sight." '

We who walk up Skiddaw as unconcernedly as we take a stroll in the park may smile; but we don't get half the pleasure those old folk got.

Saddleback, or to call it by the older, romantic name, Blencathara, is more interesting as a mountain, for it really has a bit of sharp ridge over Scales Tarn which can give a not too hardened climber the sense of mountain height. Ruskin wrote in 1867 about his walk up Saddleback, how he went up the

LOGGING AT LAKESIDE

THIRLMERE AND HELVELLYN

steep front by the central ridge to the summit. 'It is the finest thing I've yet seen,' he said – meaning in Cumberland – 'there being several bits of real crag-work, and a fine view at the top over the great plain of Penrith on one side, and the Cumberland hills, as a chain, on the other. Fine fresh wind blowing, and plenty of crows. Do you remember poor papa's favourite story about the Quaker whom the crows ate on Saddleback?' – Helvellyn, he would say, in vague remembrance of Christopher North's coarse travesty of the story which Scott and Wordsworth had told in sympathetic verse. 'There were some of the biggest and hoarsest-voiced ones about the cliff that I've ever had sympathetic croaks from: and one on the top, or near it, so big that Downes and Crawley (his servants) having Austrian tendencies in politics, took it for a "black eagle." Downes went up capitally' – Downes, when I knew him a little later, was distinctly stout – 'though I couldn't get him down again, because he *would* stop to gather ferns. However, we did it all and came down to Threlkeld – of the "Bridal of Triermain" –

> "The king his way pursued
> By lonely Threlkeld's waste and wood." '

Southerfell is the last height in the range, its name meaning not that it stands to the south, which is not the case, but

evidently like the Icelandic Saudhafall – sheep-hill: we have also Southerfield, Southerstead. It is famous for the curious mirage seen there on midsummer eve, 1735. A farm-servant thought he saw troops marching over the mountain, and of course was ridiculed for the tale. Two years later the farmer's whole family saw the same thing, and they too were thought to have gone mad. So, at midsummer, 1745, they invited a large party, and all saw an army with carriages, which could not possibly be, on the top of the fell. Next day they went to look for the footprints, but in vain. It came out that the Jacobite army had been parading or marching that evening, somewhere to the north, at a great distance; and it was supposed that this was the reflection of their figures 'by some transparent vapour, similar to the *fata morgana*.' The same thing was seen on Helvellyn on the eve of the battle of Marston Moor; and the *Lonsdale Magazine* which collected the accounts, gave a number of similar instances.

W.G. Collingwood

YANWATH HALL

THE LUCK OF EDEN HALL

A TALE OF THE MUSGRAVES

Eden Hall, the seat of the chief of the famous border clan of Musgrave, is a large and handsome edifice, on the west bank of the river Eden, built in the taste which prevailed about the time of the Charles's. Being bordered with trees, it forms an elegant feature in the pleasure grounds. There is here preserved, with scrupulous care, an old and anciently-painted glass goblet, called the 'Luck of Edenhall,' which would appear, from the following traditionary legend, to be wedded to the fortunes of its present possessors. The butler, in going to procure water at St Cuthbert's well, in the neighbourhood (rather an unusual employment for a butler) came suddenly upon a company of fairies, who were feasting and making merry on the green sward. In their flight they left behind this glass, and one of them returning for it, found it in the hands of the butler. Seeing that its recovery was hopeless, she flew away, singing aloud –

> If that glass should break or fall,
> Farewell the luck of Eden Hall.

The connection of the prosperity of the family with the integrity of an inanimate object, has frequently been one of the playthings of tradition, and traces of the superstition are found in ancient fable. There is a legend of this kind attached to a pear, preserved in a silver box at Coalstoun, the seat of the Earl of Dalhousie, near Haddington; and there is or was, a glass cap at Muncaster castle, given by Henry VI to Sir John Pennington, which, from the general opinion of the King's sanctity, and that he entailed with the gift a blessing on the family, was called 'the Luck of Muncaster.'

The initials, I.H.S., are marked upon the case containing the goblet at Eden Hall, sufficiently showing the sacred uses to which it was originally appropriated.

Wilson Armistead

Sources and Photographic Details

TEXT

The page numbers given below relate to pages in this book and not the page numbers in source books.

The sources of descriptive text are Jackson's *Ulverston and North Lonsdale Almanac & Tide Table 1885*, pp. 14–15; *Kelly's Directory for 1897*, pp. 11–12, 13, 98–101, 108, 110; W.G. Collingwood, *The Life of John Ruskin* (Methuen, London), pp. 15–16; *England's Lakeland – a tour therein* (W. Holmes Ltd, Ulverston), p. 16; J.L. Moore, *Practical Guide to the English Lake District for Pedestrians* 1886 (Abel Heywood & Son, Manchester), pp. 17–18; H.D. Rawnsley, *A coach drive at the Lakes* 1890 (T. Bakewell, Keswick), pp. 19–31, 42; A. Severn, 'Yachting on Windermere', from W.G. Collingwood's *The Lake Counties* (J.M. Dent & Co., London), pp. 31–5; Wilson Armistead, *Tales and Legends of the English Lakes* 1891 (Simpkin Marshall, London), pp. 34, 53–4, 114; *Pearson's Gossipy Guide to the English Lakes* (C.A. Pearson Ltd, London), pp. 37–9, 101, 103, 106–7; *The Official Guide to the Ullswater Steam Navigation Company* (Bemrose and Sons, Derby), pp. 40–2; *Bulmers History and Directory of Cumberland* 1901, pp. 43–8; *Proceedings of the Institute of Mechanical Engineers* 1901, p. 48; *Report of the English Lake District Association on Wyrnose–Hardknott Passes road*, pp. 49–52; F.W. Garnett, *Westmorland Agriculture – 1800–1900* (Titus Wilson, Kendal), pp. 52, 54–8, 59–63, 108; *Gates Shepherd's Guide for Cumberland, Westmorland & Lancashire*, pp. 58–9; Anne Ritchie, *Records of Tennyson, Ruskin and Browning*, 1896 (MacMillan & Co.), pp. 64–6; Mackereth of Ulverston, *Year Book 1897*, pp. 66–7, 76–81; William T. Palmer, *The English Lakes* (A. & C. Black, London), pp. 67–8; *The Girls Own Paper*, pp. 68–73; Roger Piketah, *Breks an' Haks an' sic lyk* 1902 (W. Holmes Ltd, Ulverston), pp. 74–5; Joseph Fisher, *Popular History of Barrow-in-Furness* 1891 (E.J. Frampton, Bournemouth), p. 75; *Transactions of the Cumberland & Westmorland Antiquarian and Archaeological Society*, NS 1 (1901), pp. 82–5, 104–5; Edwin Waugh, *Poesies from a Country Garden* Part II, 1866 (Simpkin Marshall, London, and John Heywood, Manchester), pp. 86–96; John Beever, *Practical Fly-fishing* 1893 (Methuen, London), pp. 96–7; Daniel Scott, *Bygone Cumberland and Westmorland* 1899 (W. Andrews & Co., London), p. 105; W.G. Collingwood, *The Lake Counties* (Warne), pp. 112–13.

Also used is *The Prospectus of the Plumgarths Hydropathic Establishment* (by courtesy of Mr and Mrs D. Wharram, Plumgarths Holiday Flats, Kendal), p. 111.

ILLUSTRATIONS

Credits and information in page order. For key to initials of sources please refer to the end of this section. Photographers where known, which include the father of Beatrix Potter, are named along with the date if recorded with the original source or where it can reasonably be deduced.

Endpapers: front, Eskdale Quarrymen *c.* 1880, Newby Bros., Barrow; JM; back, Easter, The Castle, Kendal; GD. Title page i, Pier at Ullswater; JG. Page ii, Hospital Parade on King Street, Ulverston; JG. Culgaith Fête; GD. Page iii, Boat Houses, Newby Bridge, R. Potter, 10/9/08; CA. Page iv, Building *The Lady of the Lake*, Coniston, 1908; JG. Preface, Brayton Colliery shaft bottom; AT. Furness Abbey west range, Rupert Potter 13/8/08; CA. Introduction, page 3, Carlisle Castle gatehouse, Reliable series PC; JM. Page 4, Highmoor, Wigton; JG. Page 5, Buck Hill colliery, near Great Broughton; CRA. Silloth holiday, Nicholson and Cartner, Carlisle; JM. Page 6, Freeze up at Greenodd 1895, W. Stewart; JG. Page 7, Ravenstonedale station, Yeoman of Kirkby Stephen, *c.* 1890; JM. Photographers' vans at White Moss, Rydal, Payne-Jennings; OW. Page 8, Kents Bank station; CRA. Mary Pepper lacemaking, J. Atkinson, Ulverston; AR. Title page 9, Criffel Street, Silloth; PR. Page 10, Ulverston Hospital Parade 1905; JG. Page 11, Cockermouth Main Street, J. Valentine; JM. Page 12, Brough Hill Horse Fair; JG. Carlisle Market Place, G. Bell; JM. Page 13, Sheepwashing at Mereness, Cartmel, Redhead; JG. Page 14, The Ambleside gardener, Herbert Bell; ALT. The Pepper family haymaking at Holme Ground, Tilberthwaite, Coniston; AR. Page 15, Seascale station, 1890; JG. Page 16, Wastwater, Herbert Bell; JM. John Ruskin, 1890s, Rotary Photo; JG. Page 17, Sunny Bank, Torver, Redhead; JG. Climbers on Pavey Ark, Langdale, Herbert Bell; JG. Page 18, Armathwaite, *c.* 1905; GD. Page 19, Royal celebration, Broughton-in-Furness square, 1911; JG. May Day, Temple Sowerby, 1908; JM. Page 20, Sedgwick Post Office; JM. Page 21, Mrs Turner, Kendal, 1890s, J.H. Hogg; JM. Cottage at Leece near Dalton in Furness; JG. Page 22, Watering the horses at the Kings Head, Thirlspot, *c.* 1905; JM. Page 23, Postmen at Coniston Post Office; JM. Page 24, Cottages at Cark, J. Atkinson; JM. Page 25, Bell House, Dalton, Burton-in-Kendal, Rowbotham of Burton; JM. Page 26, High Street, Whitehaven; WM. 'Awd Cooper' the Mallerstang postman, Kirkby Stephen; JM. Page 27, Whitehaven harbour in winter *c.* 1900; PR. Furness Abbey nave 13/8/1908, Rupert Potter; CA. Page 28, Crosthwaite, Keswick, Payne-Jennings; OW. Page 29, Townend, Grasmere, Redhead; JG. Page 30, The Courts, Carlisle, Reliable series PC; JM. Page 31, Yachting on Windermere, 1890s, R. & J. Brunskill; JG. Page 32, Boats for hire at Bowness Bay, Windermere 28/5/1908, Rupert Potter; CA. Page 33, Camping at Windermere; JM. Boat house on Curwen's Island, Windermere, Payne-Jennings; OW. Page 34, The pergola at the Swan Hotel, Newby Bridge; JM. Page 35, The *Teal* at the Waterhead, Ambleside Pier, 1890s, R. & J. Brunskill; JG. Page 36, Holker Hall, Cartmel, after the 1871 fire; JM. Page 37, Rose Cottage, Seathwaite, Dunnerdale, Redhead; JG. Page 38, Grasmere Pier, Payne-Jennings; OW. Two girls at Seathwaite,

Dunnerdale, Redhead; JG. Page 39, Grange in Borrowdale 3/9/1904, Rupert Potter; CA. Page 40, Off the Patterdale Pier, Ullswater 10/8/1910, Rupert Potter, CA. Page 41, Loading the Ullswater coaches, Crown Hotel, King Street, Penrith, *c.* 1902, Stengal; NH. Porter and coachman from the County Hotel, Ambleside; JM. Page 42, Church Walk, Allithwaite, Grange over Sands; JG. Page 43, Maryport and Carlisle engine at Currock Sheds, Carlisle; CRA. Page 44, Silloth harbour; AT. Page 45, Coal pickers at Brayton colliery; AT. Page 46, Kirkby in Furness slate quarry; AR. Cartmel Square about 1902, J. Atkinson; JM. Page 47, The yard at Brayton colliery; AT. Page 48, Charcoal burners near Haverthwaite; JM. Page 49, Bassenthwaite road at Keswick, 17/10/1888, Rupert Potter; CA. Santon Bridge, Redhead; JG. Page 50, Roadmen with steamroller near Longtown; MS. By coach in Ravenglass, the Photochrom Co.; JM. Page 51, Building Shopford bridge at the Limekiln Inn, Bewcastle; BS. Page 52, Keekle Terrace, Cleator; JM. Page 53, Main Street, Kirkby Lonsdale, J. Sawyers, Kendal; JM. The Llewellyn Davies memorial in Kirkby Lonsdale Square, *c.* 1906; JM. Page 54, Hesket Show 1905; JM. Page 55, Kendal Horse Fair; GD. With the horse at Fellgate, Woodland, Coniston, Redhead; JG. Page 56, Shearing at Mansrigg, Ulverston; JG. Jane Routledge Goodfellow Lauder at Woodside, Bewcastle; BS. Page 57, Sheepshearing at Bainsbank, Middleton, Kirkby Lonsdale; OW. Page 58, Wythburn and Helvellyn from The City, Thirlmere, 10/9/1897, Rupert Potter; CA. Page 59, Rose Cottage, Bailey, Bewcastle; BS. Page 60, Kirkby Thore; JM. Page 61, Oakshaw, Clattering Ford, Bewcastle; IG. Crookburn Foot, Bailey, Bewcastle; BS. Page 62, West Cumberland Harvest; PR. Page 63, Threshing at Selside Hall, nr Kendal; HLH, Traction engine near Broughton-in-Furness, 1880s, Newby Bros.; JM. Page 64, Tilberthwaite Farm, Coniston; AR. Page 65, Fellgate cottage and garden, Woodland, Redhead; JG. Page 66, Duddon Hall gardens, Redhead; JG. Page 67, The Oxenhope pack of Otter Hounds, Dallam, Milnthorpe; JG. Page 68, Cochrane's cart outside Keen's shop, Netherby Street, Longtown; BS. Page 69, Little Langdale School; AR. Abigail Pepper spinning at Holme Ground, Tilberthwaite, Langdale Linen Industry, J. Atkinson; JM. Page 70, Elizabeth Pepper at the loom, Langdale Linen Industry, J. Atkinson; JM. Page 71, Caldbeck bobbin mill; JG. Page 72, On the fell near Burton-in-Kendal – the slipper rock, Rowbotham of Burton; JM. Broughton Mills, Redhead; JG. Page 73, Near Duddon Hall, Redhead; JG. Page 74, 'Fond of his Licker' on the steamers at Barrow; JM. Page 75, Egremont procession, Baker; JM. Page 76, Ensign and Mrs Clifford, Salvation Army, Barrow-in-Furness, Hargreaves; JG. Wedding of Miss C.B. Knowles of Broughton Lodge and Revd J.A. Nash of Tunstall at Field Broughton Church, Cartmel 20/6/1906, Mrs Sutcliffe of Burton in Kendal; JM. Page 77, Eva Phillips, the 1908 Rose Queen Ulverston Hospital Saturday parade; JG. Wedding at Derwent Hill, Portinscale, Keswick; JM. Page 78, Mr and Mrs Coward of Foxfield, Broughton-in-Furness 1885, Stewart; JM. Page 79, The Fairer family in the garden at Highfield, Shap; JF. Page 80, The Woodside children, Wigton; JM. Sailor boy at Barrow-in-Furness, Davis; JG. Page 81, Three girls at Fellgate, Woodland,

Coniston, Redhead; JG. Page 82, Nunnery Walks, Kirkoswald, Whitehead of Appleby; GD. Marbles at Arnside, Crosland; JM. Page 83, Arthuret Church, Longtown choir boys with the Revd Ivor Graham at Crow Wood on the Glebe; MS. Page 84, 'Settling old scores at Yearngill', near Aspatria; AT. Billy Bumley House, Workington; JM. Page 85, Highfield, Workington; JM. Flag Street, Hawkshead, 1890s, Alfred Pettitt; JM. Page 86, Lady's Cottage, Conishead, Ulverston, Braithwaite; JG. Page 87, Greenodd Sands; JG. Fishing at Foxfield; JG. Page 88, Market Street, Ulverston, Smith; JG. Page 89, J.W. Croft's Grayrigg Smithy, nr Kendal. J. Sawyers; JM. Page 90, Ship Inn, Sandside, Milnthorpe, G. Wilson of Grange over Sands; JM. Sandside, Kirkby-in-Furness. H. Simcoe of Kendal; JM. Page 91, Kirkby-in-Furness from the shore, Sankey; JG. Page 92, Mr Preston at Skelwith Farm, Redhead; JG. Page 93, Cartmel Priory, 17/8/1908, Rupert Potter; CA. Page 94, Natland Church, nr Kendal, H. Simcoe; JM. Page 95, Derwent Bay, Keswick, 8/9/1897, Rupert Potter; CA. Page 96, Boating at Grasmere, Redhead; JG. Page 97, Highgate, Kendal 1880s; JM. Page 98, Longtown schoolchildren with their headmaster Mr Black, MS. Annie Hodgson and Elizabeth Farrel of Longtown, Plenderleith; MS. Page 99, Building the tramway near the Courts on the Crescent, Carlisle; CRA. Page 100, Carlisle Citadel station, 1890s; CRA. Midland Railway train at Carlisle, 1910; CRA. Page 101, Warwick Road, Carlisle; CRA. Page 102, Ambleside Centre (site of the bus station), Payne-Jennings; OW. Prince of Wales, Grasmere, 1890s; JM. Page 103, Pony ride at the Prince of Wales Hotel, Grasmere 1890s; JM. The Hornby family take tea with the Vicar at Dalton Hall Tea-room, Burton-in-Kendal 1890s, Mrs Sutcliffe, Burton; JM. Page 104, Lodore Hotel, Derwentwater, Keswick 1890s; JM. Page 105, Crosby Ravensworth; JM. Old Pump Inn, Kendal, Atkinson & Pollitt; GD. Page 106, *Britannia* fires a salute for the 1897 Jubilee celebration, Windermere, J. Brunskill; JG. Top of Honister Pass at the turn of the century, Alfred Pettitt, Keswick; JM. Page 107, Spark Bridge panorama, Redhead; JG. Paddling in the Derwent, Borrowdale, Keswick; JM. Page 108, St Luke's Fair, Kirkby Stephen; GD. Page 109, Ambleside rushbearing; JM. Grasmere rushbearing; JM. Page 110, Mr and Mrs J. Fairer's wedding party at the Weslyan Chapel, Shap, 21/7/1898; JF. Page 111, Cropper Memorial Hospital, Kendal, J. Ewan; GD. Page 112, Logging at Lakeside, 5/8/1902, Rupert Potter; CA. Page 113, Thirlmere and Helvellyn with new draw off tower and road under construction, 22/9/1898, Rupert Potter; CA. Page 114, Yanwath Hall, near Penrith, 19/8/1897, Rupert Potter; CA.

KEY: ALT, The Armitt (Library) Trust, Ambleside; AR, Abigail Reed, Kendal; AT, Anne U. Thomas, Seaton; BS, Barbara Smith, Roadhead; CA, Kendal Record Office, Cumbria Archives; CRA, Cumbrian Railways Association; GD, George Dawson (N. Carradice collection), Kendal; HLH, Holme Local History Society; IG, Iver Gray, Longtown; JF. John Fairer, Shap; JG, John Garbutt, Allithwaite; JM, John Marsh, Kendal; MS, Marlene Storey, Longtown; NH, Neil Honeyman, Barrow-in-Furness; OW, Olive Wilson, Calgarth; PR, Peter Robinson, Grange over Sands; WM, Whitehaven Museum.